Leadership on the Line

The Workbook

A Self-Study or Group-Led Companion Piece to

Leadership on the Line

A Guide for Front Line Supervisors,
Business Owners, and Emerging Leaders

By
Ed Rehkopf

CLARITY PUBLICATIONS

Mooresville, North Carolina

Also by Ed Rehkopf

Leadership on the Line: A Guide for Front Line Supervisors, Business Owners, and Emerging Leaders

The Quest for Remarkable Service

Service-Based Leadership Transforms Your Hospitality Operation

What I Expect from My Club Management Team

<u>*On-the-Go Training Series*</u>
Management Disciplines on the Go
Food Service Management on the Go
Leadership on the Go
Values on the Go
Service on the Go
Employee Development and Disciplinary Guides on the Go
Human Resources on the Go
Accounting on the Go

In Praise of *Leadership on the Line—The Workbook*

"Hard to believe, but *The Workbook* is even better than the book! Taken together they form an incredibly useful tool to help train my managers and supervisors to a consistent conception and application of leadership at our club."

Chris Conner, General Manager
The River Club

"I finished reading *The Workbook* over the weekend. It is a great read. I wish there was a way to give this information out to all would-be or up-and-coming General Managers."

Michelle M. Cook, Dir. of Marketing & Vendor Relationships
International Club Suppliers

"Generally, books written about leadership are designed to instruct readers to be more effective leaders; however, these books rarely afford an opportunity for self-assessment. By creating this workbook as a companion piece to *Leadership on the Line*, the author has created a perfect union between theory and application. As I progressed through *The Workbook*, I tried to be completely honest with myself in assessing my strengths and weaknesses, which proved to be an eye-opening experience. Reading *Leadership on the Line* and completing *The Workbook* will be a requirement for all of my managers."

Saeed Assadzandi, General Manager
Champion Hills Country Club

"Although not new to leadership positions, I found myself moving through *The Workbook* with anticipation and, with each response to the exercises, there came an enlightened sense of how I could become a better leader."

Jennifer C. Wichowski, CMCA
Regional General Manager

Most leadership books are written for mid-level managers aspiring to senior positions. Few are written to address the challenges of first-time or front-line managers and supervisors. Those that do usually focus on technical skills, not leadership. Yet it is the junior manager who so often directs a company's customer-facing employees. Without strong, consistent leadership at this level to direct, motivate, and inspire employees, a company's customer service efforts will certainly be at risk.

Leadership on the Line—The Workbook addresses this need by explaining in simple, easy-to-understand terms the requirements of Service-Based Leadership—a style of leadership based on the need to develop strong relationships with followers and focused on serving the needs of all constituencies—boss, customers, peers, and employees. With Service-Based Leadership customers are treated well because employees are valued, trained, supported, and empowered by their leaders.

The Workbook takes the concepts spelled out in *Leadership on the Line: A Guide from Front Line Supervisors, Business Owners, and Emerging Leaders* and breaks them down into easy-to-absorb lessons for those just starting on the path to successful leadership. As such it is the perfect training tool for young managers and those who must direct them. The most frequent comment heard from senior leaders about *Leadership on the Line* is, "I wish I had read something like this years ago."

Leadership on the Line
The Workbook

Acknowledgement

Special thanks to my wife Clara for her invaluable editorial assistance, as well as her many helpful insights into the content and formatting of this Workbook. I would also like to thank Michelle Cook, Director of Marketing and Vendor Relations for International Club Suppliers/Entegra Procurement Services, and Chris Conner, General Manager of The River Club in Suwanee, Georgia, for their careful reading of the manuscript and helpful suggestions to improve the substance and impact of the material.

Printing History:

1st Printing—November 2009
2nd Printing—December 2012

Copyright 2009
Ed Rehkopf
All Rights Reserved

With the exception of the Boss Assessment on pages 86-89, this work may not be reproduced in whole or in part in any media (print, electronic, or otherwise) without the express permission of the author.

ISBN 10: 0-9722193-2-3
ISBN 13: 978-0-9722193-2-7

Printed and bound in the United States of America by
RJ Communications, New York

*To my daughters,
Kate, Meghan, Carrie Nye, and Foley,
who have given me much joy and love.*

BORN OR MADE?—

"The most dangerous leadership myth is that leaders are born—that there is a genetic factor to leadership. This myth asserts that people simply either have certain charismatic qualities or not. That's nonsense; in fact, the opposite is true. Leaders are made rather than born."

                    Warren G. Bennis
                    American scholar, organizational consultant and author, widely regarded as a pioneer in the field of contemporary Leadership Studies

Leadership on the Line
The Workbook

Introduction 1

Leadership Basics
    Your Role 5
    Your Constituencies 6
    Service-Based Leadership 7
    Good Leadership—It's Just Common Sense 8
    Leadership Principles 9
    Leadership Traits 10
    Good Leadership Examples 11
    Bad Bosses May Damage Your Heart 12
    Fear-Based Management 13
    Poor Leadership Examples 14
    Strengths and Weaknesses 15
    What You Dislike Doing 16
    Overcoming Obstacles 17
    Learning from Failure 18

Leadership Values
    Management Professionalism 22
    Exercise #1 24
    Managers' Code of Ethics 25
    Exercise #2 26
    Principles of Employee Relations 27
    Exercise #3 28

Leadership Lessons
    Authority, Responsibility, Accountability 32
    Relationships 33
    Charisma and Trust 34
    Consistency and Common Decency 35
    Exercise #4 36
    Active and Engaged Leadership 37
    Our Need to Serve 39
    The Hierarchy of Service 40
    Ego-Driven Failure 42
    Leadership Growth and Adaptation 43
    Projecting Confidence 44

THE SPINNING TOP—

Business operations are like rotating tops. Without the daily spin of leadership, they soon begin to wobble and fall down.

Table of Contents

    Personal Responsibility 45
    Leadership and a Failure of Engagement 46
    Exercise #5 47
    Morale Matters 48
    Do the Right Thing 49
    Value Your People 51

Leadership Applications
    What You Owe Your Boss—Loyalty and Support 56
    Managing Your Boss 57
    Disciplined Hiring 58
    Why the Wrong People Are Hired 59
    Creating a Lasting Organizational Culture 61
    Standards, Policies, and Procedures 63
    Training 65
    Personal Productivity 67
    Planning and Review 69
    Continual Process Improvement 70
    Managers' Fiscal Responsibilities 71
    Benchmarking 73
    Performance Reviews 74
    Exercise #6 76
    Steps to Lower Employee Turnover 77
    Employee Empowerment 78
    The Distinction between Empowerment and Discretion 79
    The Many Ways to "Kill" Empowerment 80

Leadership Assessments
    Training Assessment 84
    Exercise #7 85
    The Boss Assessment 86
    The Personal Assessment 90
    Your Leadership Assessment 91
    Developing A Leadership Plan 93
    Exercise #8 94

Conclusion 95
Bibliography 97

EMPLOYEE RELATIONS—

"The number one impact on customer relations is employee relations—happy employees create happy customers."

    Chip R. Bell and
    John R. Patterson
    Customer Service
    Consultants

Leadership on the Line
The Workbook

PURPOSE

The Workbook is intended to be an introduction to the basics of leadership for front line supervisors, emerging leaders, and even business owners who wish to enhance their enterprise's performance through improved employee engagement and empowerment. Easy to read and grasp, it lays out the foundation upon which a career of successful leadership can be built.

The Workbook, like the book, is not meant to be the last word on leadership, nor does it cover all aspects of a subject that is easily a lifelong pursuit. Rather it is intended to provide in simple terms the requirements of Service-Based Leadership and the skills necessary to establish successful relationships between the leader and constituencies at the level of contact with the customer.

BACKGROUND

Since the first publication of *Leadership on the Line* in 2002, readers have suggested that we prepare a workbook to accompany the text. Given the frequent comment that the book, while easy-to-read, contained a lot of key leadership advice, the consensus was that the material needed to be absorbed in smaller, more in-depth doses.

This workbook is designed to guide the reader through the concepts of leadership at a more thoughtful and personal pace, allowing each individual to focus on those issues where he or she recognizes the need for improvement, while moving more quickly through areas of recognized competence.

SELF-STUDY OR GUIDED INSTRUCTION

The Workbook has been designed to be used as either a self-study guide for an individual trying to improve his or her leadership skills or as a manual for an instructor to guide a group of students through the process. In both cases, *The Workbook* provides detailed guidance to the individual or instructor to help get the most out of the experience.

Ultimately though, as with any form of learning, the individual student will benefit from *The Workbook* only in direct proportion to the effort he or she puts into it.

BECOMING A SERVICE-BASED LEADER

Developing leadership skills is not memorizing a list of things to do or not to do, though such lists are useful in helping students learn. Leadership is not the accumulation of managerial abilities, such as budgeting, computer skills, or the specific work skills of a particular industry, though such aptitudes will certainly enhance your overall skill set and add to your competence. Leadership is not a position or a title.

Successful leadership depends on the **quality of relationships between a leader and followers**. As such it entails relationship skills—the personal characteristics and abilities to connect with and inspire the enthusiastic efforts of a diverse group of people toward a common goal.

True leadership requires an understanding of what makes people tick—individually and in group settings. It requires sensitivity to the needs and desires of others, even when they may not be able to adequately define or communicate these themselves. It requires openness and accessibility so followers are comfortable bringing their concerns and issues to the leader. It requires a person who is self-analytical, who

---

FAILING ORGANIZATIONS—

"Failing organizations are usually over-managed and under-led."

Warren G. Bennis
Leadership Expert

© 2009—Ed Rehkopf

Introduction

examines every less-than-optimum outcome for improvement, often discovering a better way to interact with followers. It requires a person who puts the needs of the enterprise ahead of personal ambition, who recognizes that tending to the group welfare in a disciplined way will ultimately bring about better performance.

Finally, learning leadership skills is not a one-time event. Just as different endeavors and levels of organizations require different skill sets for managerial success, leadership skills must expand and develop as the individual moves up to higher levels of responsibility. Satisfactory leadership skills in a front line supervisory position are clearly inadequate for the challenges of a general manager, division manager, or president of a company. But the skills learned in the early years of one's career will be the foundation for the broader skills necessary when one takes on greater responsibilities, particularly if you understand that true leadership is a lifelong journey, not a destination.

THE SINGLE MOST IMPORTANT REQUIREMENT TO BECOMING A SERVICE-BASED LEADER

Becoming a Service-Based Leader is a transformative process; it's about personal growth. The student must be prepared to challenge ingrained attitudes and beliefs about self and others. It requires a willingness to closely examine motivations and habits. The emerging leader must also be willing to accept personal responsibility for his or her life and decisions. But most of all it requires **a great deal of personal honesty**. Self-delusion and denial are the committed enemies of personal growth.

As you progress through *The Workbook*, make a promise to yourself. Promise that you will search the depths of your being to get to and understand your deepest motivations, not those that you glibly repeat because you have so often heard others say them and think they're the norm. True leadership is not the norm, and becoming an effective leader will require you to step outside your comfort zone and confront the beliefs and attitudes you hold, not from conviction but from unexamined habit.

THE REWARDS OF SERVICE-BASED LEADERSHIP

Developing the skills of a Service-Based Leader will reward you in a variety of ways. First and foremost, I believe the foundation of Service-Based Leadership and a recognition of the value of people in all you do, can, over the course of a career, lead you to the Level 5 Leadership that Jim Collins found at the top of all *Good to Great* companies.

Second, because Service-Based Leadership is all about developing successful relationships, it can bring success to other parts of your life—your family relationships, your friendships, and the way you interact with people wherever you meet them.

Lastly, Service-Based Leadership will help you develop the self-analytical skills to examine life's challenges and better understand how you react to them. Ultimately, it will help you to grow as a person and learn to face difficulties with greater equanimity and purpose.

PROFILE OF A LEADER IN TROUBLE—

- Has a poor understanding of people.
- Lacks imagination.
- Has personal problems.
- Passes the buck.
- Feels secure and satisfied.
- Is not organized.
- Flies into rages.
- Will not take risks.
- Is insecure and defensive.
- Stays inflexible.
- Has no team spirit.
- Fights change.

John C. Maxwell
Developing the Leader Within You

© 2009—Ed Rehkopf

INFLUENCE—

"The key to successful leadership today is influence, not authority."

Ken Blanchard
Author and Management Expert

Leadership on the Line
The Workbook

THE BASICS—

Hopefully, you've already read *Leadership on the Line, A Guide for Front Line Supervisors, Business Owners, and Emerging Leaders.* The book lays the foundation for what will follow in *The Workbook.* While not a prerequisite, it would make you much more familiar with some of the concepts we'll cover here.

In this first section, we will focus on the basics of leadership and ask you to examine your attitudes and beliefs about those basics. This is important as a starting point for the remaining sections of this workbook.

Your Role	5
Your Constituencies	6
Service-Based Leadership	7
Good Leadership—It's Just Common Sense	8
Leadership Principles	9
Leadership Traits	10
Good Leadership Examples	11
Bad Bosses May Damage Your Heart	12
Fear-Based Management	13
Poor Leadership Examples	14
Strengths and Weaknesses	15
What You Dislike Doing	16
Overcoming Obstacles	17
Learning from Failure	18

Leadership Basics

Leadership on the Line
The Workbook

Your Role

Name: _____

Title: _____

To whom do you report? _____

Approximately how many people report to you? _____

Do you have bottom-line responsibility for your department or section?
☐ Yes ☐ No

What is your department/section's mission? _____
_____
_____
_____

List your primary duties: _____
_____
_____
_____
_____
_____
_____
_____
_____
_____
_____
_____
_____
_____
_____
_____
_____

BOTTOM-LINE RESPONSIBILITY—

Bottom-line responsibility is the financial accountability that a manager has for the operation or portion of the operation for which he or she is responsible.

The General Manager has bottom line responsibility for the entire operation. A Department Head—say the Food and Beverage Director—is responsible for the bottom line performance of the F&B Department.

Figuratively, the term bottom-line responsibility has come to signify the absolute accountability a manager has for everything under his or her supervision.

© 2009—Ed Rehkopf

Basics

WHO ARE YOUR CONSTITUENCIES?

"Before you can effectively exercise your leadership skills, you must clearly recognize your various constituencies—those groups who depend on you and for whom you must provide leadership and service. For many positions this is fairly clear cut; there are customers, employees, and a boss. However, for some positions there may be other groups who rely upon your exercise of leadership.

So for every leadership position, one must identify the constituencies served. Once you have identified these, make a list of each constituency's needs and how you and/or your team can best serve them. In most cases you need to visit with constituents to hear directly from them what they need or expect from you.

With a clear understanding of their needs, you are in a far better position to determine priorities and execute your responsibilities."

Leadership on the Line

Your Constituencies

Every leader serves multiple constituencies—"those groups who depend on you and for whom you must provide leadership and service." These constituencies typically fall into three groups—"customers, employees, and a boss."

List and explain what things your constituencies depend upon you for:

1. Customers: _____

2. Employees: _____

3. Boss: _____

4. Others: _____

© 2009—Ed Rehkopf

Leadership on the Line
The Workbook

LEADERSHIP—

"Given that [Leadership] ultimately involves guiding, influencing, and directing people, I posit the following working definition for this book:

Leadership is the sum of those individual traits, skills, and abilities that allow one person to commit and direct the efforts of others toward the accomplishment of a particular objective.

Central to this definition is the understanding that exercising leadership involves building and sustaining relationships between leader and followers. Without this bond or connection, there are no willing followers and, therefore, no true leader. Given that no leader operates in a vacuum, it also requires the leader to establish relationships with other relevant constituencies."

Leadership on the Line

© 2009—Ed Rehkopf

Service-Based Leadership

"With Service-Based Leadership, the attitude and primary motivation of the leader is service to others—to customers, to employees, to shareholders. This approach to leadership **naturally creates relationships**—the deep and abiding bonds that sustain the efforts of the company. This outward focus of the leader sets up a dynamic where:

- Employees are continually recognized.
- There is an open flow of ideas, opinions, and information.
- Initiative and risk are highly regarded.
- Problem discovery and solution is a focus while placing blame is unimportant.
- Every employee feels energized and part of the team and is valued for his or her contribution.
- Prestige is derived from performance and contribution, not title or position.
- Customers are treated well because employees are treated well.
- The energy and initiative of all employees is focused on the common effort.

With Service-Based Leadership, you will find that service to both internal and external customers is effortless. Less energy is expended in processing complaints, grievances, and conflicts. Work is more fun and everyone's job is easier.

Serving Your Constituencies

The key to serving the needs of those you serve lies in ensuring that you **build strong relationships** with individuals. How do you do this? Begin by:

- Treating everyone you meet with courtesy, respect, and good cheer.
- Focusing on each person you deal with as if he or she were the most important person in the world.
- Taking the time to get to know people; sharing your time and attention with them.
- Learning about other people's jobs and the challenges and the difficulties they face.
- Keeping promises and following through on commitments.
- Being principled, showing fairness, and demonstrating integrity.
- Recognizing the ultimate value of people in all you do.

Relationships depend upon how you view yourself in relation to others. If you see yourself as separate and apart from your constituencies, if you view others as the means to your ends, if your vision and goals lack a broader purpose than your own needs and ambitions, establishing meaningful relationships will be impossible. On the other hand, **when you see yourself as part of a team with a shared mission, then a sense of service will be an intrinsic part of your service team relationships.**"

Leadership on the Line

Basics

Good Leadership—It's Just Common Sense

CUSTOMER SERVICE TRAINING—

I recently read an Internet-posted news article entitled, "Disney Offers Customer Service Training." Written by Adrian Sainz, the article talked about Miami International Airport employees taking customer service training from the Disney Institute, a division of Walt Disney Company set up to teach its principles and practices to other companies. Let's pick up on the story at right.

"Now the Institute has taken another client: Miami International Airport, which many travelers will tell you needs customer service training like an airplane needs wings. Surveys rank its service among the nation's worst. The airport's terminal operations employees are taking classes taught by Institute instructors, learning leadership practices, team building, staff relations and communication skills—many formulated by Walt Disney himself.

Disney takes great pride in ensuring a fun time and repeat business, mainly by emphasizing customer service and attention to detail while trying not to appear too sterile or robotic.

Early in the training, a handful of Miami airport managers visited the Magic Kingdom, where they were shown examples on how paying attention to detail and removing barriers were integral in making guests happy and keeping them informed."

The article went on discussing various techniques used by Disney to enhance customer service. While I found this discussion somewhat interesting, it was the reader comments posted below the article that caught my attention. Here they are:

> 1st Posted Comment: "I work for a medical practice in Georgia that sends a few of their employees to Disney for training each year. Our patients (guests) really responded well to our new customer service guidelines. However, management really needed to attend the training as well as the regular employees. They became complacent in their 'ivory tower' and expected all of us to treat the patients well (and of course we did); however, **management needed to extend the same courtesy and good manners to their employees.** In the past 3 months the company has had record turnover and still harbors a large disgruntled employee pool. No idle words .... **'Treat others the way you would want to be treated.'**"

> 2nd Posted Comment: "When we returned, all 1st level management (the ones dealing with the customers) were asked to implement the Disney experience in our daily activities. To this day we have weekly meetings with our senior management to report how our teams are embracing the changes. Unfortunately many of the associates treat it as 'the flavor of the month' program to improve customer satisfaction. We are still trying to make a culture change with our staff. **The most unfortunate part of the Disney experience was that although our senior management went along on the trip, I am yet to witness the impact it had on them when dealing with us 1st level managers.**"

> 3rd Posted Comment: "I agree with the posters who feel that **senior management should lead by example and treat their subordinates with dignity and respect. It just seems like common sense, that when employees are happy and feel well treated, this will filter down to the way they treat the customers. Everyone in an organization deserves to be treated well and this makes for optimum performance.**"

Three of the four postings by readers made the same point about management. This suggests the obvious: that without the active involvement and example of leadership (and Service-Based Leadership at that), improvements in employee morale, dedication, empowerment, and ultimately in customer service will not happen.

© 2009—Ed Rehkopf

Leadership on the Line
The Workbook

DEFINITION—

A principle is a rule or code of conduct.

LEADERSHIP PRINCIPLES—

- "Be professionally and technically proficient.
- Respect and show concern for those you lead.
- Set the example.
- Know your capabilities and seek self-improvement.
- Understand your mission.
- Communicate your expectations.
- Instill motivation and morale in those you lead.
- Build teamwork.
- Make sound and timely decisions.
- Develop your subordinates.
- Ensure tasks are understood, properly supervised, and accomplished.
- Be responsible for your actions."

Leadership on the Line

© 2009—Ed Rehkopf

Leadership Principles

Select two of the Leadership Principles listed in the sidebar and explain in your own words why the principle is important to both the leader and his followers.

Example: **Selected Principle:** <u>Set the example</u>
Leader: <u>If I am going to lead others, I must be prepared to lead by example. My followers must see that I am prepared to do that which I ask of them. Such example helps form and reinforce my moral authority to lead.</u>
Follower: <u>I would lose respect for my leader if he did not "practice what he preaches." Without that respect it would be hard for me to trust him and be a willing and committed follower.</u>

Selected Principle: _____

Leader: _____
_____
_____
_____

Follower: _____
_____
_____
_____
_____

Selected Principle: _____

Leader: _____
_____
_____
_____

Follower: _____
_____
_____
_____
_____

Basics

DEFINITION—

A trait is a distinguishing quality or personal characteristic.

LEADERSHIP TRAITS—

- "The will to make things happen.
- Willingness to take and stand by an unpopular view.
- The ability to pace oneself and go the distance.
- Loyalty to the company, superiors, and employees.
- Willingness to make decisions based upon the best available information and analysis.
- Dependability and consistency.
- Integrity and truthfulness.
- Fairness.
- Good judgment.
- Willingness to share praise and shoulder blame.
- Professional decorum, understanding the correct time and place for everything.
- Enthusiasm."

Leadership on the Line

© 2009—Ed Rehkopf

Leadership Traits

In your own words, explain the importance of the following leadership traits. In discussing, consider both the importance to the company and to employees.

The will to make things happen:

_____
_____
_____
_____
_____
_____
_____

Integrity and truthfulness:

_____
_____
_____
_____
_____
_____
_____

Enthusiasm:

_____
_____
_____
_____
_____
_____
_____

Leadership on the Line
The Workbook

BEHAVIORAL EXAMPLES—

We have all worked for bosses in our lives, and their examples, both good and bad, can teach us much about becoming true leaders.

Hopefully, you have worked for some good leaders or had the opportunity to observe good leaders in action.

List some of the things you have seen or experienced that constituted good leadership and how they motivated or energized you to work harder or do better.

Use any example you can think of and search for what you found impressive about the behavior. How can these examples influence your own current work environment?

© 2009—Ed Rehkopf

Good Leadership Examples

Examples of good leadership and how it made you feel.

Example: *My boss shook my hand yesterday in front of my co-workers and told me what a great job I had done. I was both surprised and thrilled that she recognized my efforts. Doing it publicly made it even better.*

1 _____

2 _____

List two things that you could do as a leader to create better work relationships with your employees.

Example: *Make myself available and approachable for my employees by spending a little time talking to each one every day.*

1 _____

2 _____

Basics

Bad Bosses May Damage Your Heart

"Feeling undervalued can cause stress. Inconsiderate bosses not only make work stressful, they may also increase the risk of heart disease for their employees, experts believe.

A Swedish team found **a strong link between poor leadership and the risk of serious heart disease and heart attacks** among more than 3,000 employed men. And the effect may be cumulative—the risk went up the longer an employee worked for the same company. The study is published in *Occupational and Environmental Medicine*.

Experts said that feeling undervalued and unsupported at work can cause stress, which often fosters unhealthy behaviors, such as smoking, that can lead to heart disease. Previous work has shown that unfair bosses can drive up their employees' blood pressure, and persistent high blood pressure can increase heart disease risk.

For the latest study, researchers from the Karolinska Institute and Stockholm University tracked the heart health of the male employees, aged between 19 and 70 and working in the Stockholm area, over a period of nearly a decade. During this time 74 cases of fatal and non-fatal heart attack or acute angina, or death from ischaemic heart disease, occurred.

All the participants were asked to rate the leadership style of their senior managers on competencies such as how clearly they set out goals for their staff and how good they were at communicating and giving feedback.

The staff who deemed their senior managers to be the least competent had a 25% higher risk of a serious heart problem. And those working for what was classed as a long time—four years or more—had a 64% higher risk. The findings held true, regardless of educational attainment, social class, income, workload, lifestyle factors, such as smoking and exercise, and other risk factors for heart disease, such as high blood pressure and diabetes.

The researchers, which included experts from University College London in the UK and the Finnish Institute of Occupational Health, said that if a direct cause and effect was confirmed, then managers' behavior should be targeted in a bid to stave off serious heart disease among less senior employees. They said managers should give employees clear work objectives and **sufficient power** in relation to their responsibilities.

Cathy Ross, cardiac nurse for the British Heart Foundation, said: 'This limited, male-only study suggests that a **good, clear working relationship** with your manager may help to protect against heart disease.'

'Feeling undervalued and unsupported can cause stress, which often leads to unhealthy behaviors such as smoking, eating a poor diet, drinking too much alcohol and not getting enough exercise—adding to your risk of developing heart problems.'"

BBC News, November 25, 2008

REAL REPERCUSSIONS—

I came across this news item on the Internet and found it interesting that science has apparently found a link between health and the type of boss you work for.

My personal experience and that of many of my friends, colleagues, and acquaintances is that there are far more "bad" bosses out there than there are good ones. With all the attention given to healthier lifestyles these days, we should all question the true cost of poor leadership, both in terms of healthcare expenses and quality of life. A 64% higher risk for heart attack is a significant matter!

The good news is that something fairly simple can be done. Good leadership is a matter of good relationships. It's following the Golden Rule. Anybody can learn to be a better leader. It's a matter of examining one's attitudes about others and applying oneself to modifying behaviors.

© 2009—Ed Rehkopf

Leadership on the Line
The Workbook

FEAR-BASED MANAGEMENT—

"Fear-based management is rooted in the insecurities of the supervisor. While most people have insecurities, in this instance, the immature, inexperienced, and untrusting attitude of the supervisor dominates the workplace. Some symptoms of fear-based management are:

- Unwillingness to take a risk.
- Lack of initiative and acceptance of the status quo.
- Employees afraid to express opinions or answer questions.
- Lack of trust.
- Defensiveness and blame placing.
- Lack of communication or only top-down communication.
- Poor motivation and morale.

Fear-based management can be overcome by a leader with an open, trusting attitude and a willingness to grow, both as a person and a leader. Because of its detrimental impact on employees, customers, and the bottom line, fear-based management should not be tolerated in any company."

Leadership on the Line

© 2009—Ed Rehkopf

Fear-Based Management

Select two of the symptoms of Fear-Based Management listed in the sidebar and explain in your own words why the symptom is detrimental to both the leader and her followers.

Example: **Selected Symptom:** *Defensiveness and blame placing.*
Leader: *A leader who refuses to accept personal responsibility for her operation will constantly and continually blame others for her failures.*
Follower: *Employees quickly recognize a leader who is defensive and blames others, including her employees, for all the operation's problems. Blaming others for one's failures is a quick way to destroy the trust that underlies interpersonal relationships and will quickly alienate followers.*

Selected Symptom: _____

Leader: _____

Follower: _____

Selected Symptom: _____

Leader: _____

Follower: _____

Basics

Poor Leadership Examples

List the offending behavior and how it made you feel.

Example: *My manager yelled at me in front of customers.*
I was humiliated in front of both co-workers and customers.

1 _____

2 _____

For each offending behavior you listed above, tell how the situation could have been handled differently from a Service-Based Leadership standpoint.

Example: *Since my manager yelled at me for something that I was never shown how to do, he should take responsibility for doing a better and more consistent job of training employees. Secondly, if an employee makes a mistake, any discussion or correction should be in private with the emphasis on correcting the problem, not punishing or humiliating the employee.*

1 _____

2 _____

BEHAVIORAL EXAMPLES—

Stop and think about the poor leaders you have worked for and what they did or didn't do that created problems for you or made you less willing to give the job your total effort. After listing the offending behaviors at the top of the page, think deeply about how these behaviors made you feel, how they de-motivated you, or created problems for, or possibly between, you and your fellow workers.

If you can't think of any, maybe you have heard tales from others—your friends or relatives. Possibly you've witnessed an interchange between an employee and boss at a restaurant you've frequented or while shopping at the mall. Use any example you can think of and search for what you found offensive about the behavior. Then consider how a Service-Based approach could have created a more positive outcome.

© 2009—Ed Rehkopf

Leadership on the Line
The Workbook

Strengths and Weaknesses

List your perceived strengths and weaknesses as a leader and manager.

Strengths	Weaknesses
_____	_____
_____	_____
_____	_____
_____	_____
_____	_____
_____	_____
_____	_____
_____	_____
_____	_____
_____	_____

STRENGTHS AND WEAKNESSES—

We are the best judges of what we do well and what we could improve upon. Honestly assessing strengths and weaknesses leads to understanding.

An understanding of strengths and weaknesses helps you to better identify mentors, training programs, self-help courses, reading material, or other resources to strengthen weak areas.

Further, a better understanding of strengths and weaknesses allows you to involve yourself in projects and initiatives where your strengths will be most evident, while minimizing the impact of any weaknesses.

As you progress through your career, periodically examine your strengths and weaknesses to better understand what you may need to work on.

© 2009—Ed Rehkopf

Basics

What You Dislike Doing

List aspects of your job that you dislike. Be specific. The more accurately you can identify them, the better able you will be to work on strengthening your leadership skill set.

_____

_____

_____

_____

_____

_____

_____

_____

_____

_____

_____

DISLIKES—

The things you dislike about your job are clear pointers for work relationships that need to be examined. When there is something you dread doing, it usually has to do with difficult work relationships or areas where your leadership or management skills need work.

We all like to do those things at which we excel, while avoiding or putting off those things we don't enjoy. A better understanding of why you dislike some aspect of your job should help you figure out what needs work.

Example: Say you get angry with employees who are not performing well or whose conduct in the workplace is inappropriate. This dislike may be due to your discomfort in confronting others, or it may point to a need for better training of your staff. In either case, by identifying the problem you are better able to come up with a suitable fix for the issue.

As with strengths and weaknesses, your dislikes will change over time. A periodic assessment will help clearly identify what needs work and what your improvement priorities should be.

© 2009—Ed Rehkopf

The Workbook

OBSTACLES AND HANDICAPS—

Leaders will always find themselves facing obstacles and handicaps as they attempt to complete their mission. It is these challenges that measure your success as a leader and problem-solver. They should be addressed with enthusiasm and resolve.

List an obstacle or handicap you feel impedes your progress and performance and then list what steps you might take to overcome it.

Overcoming Obstacles

Example: My budget does not allow me to staff appropriately to provide the expected levels of service during all hours of operation.

Steps to Overcome:
1) By better organizing my work areas, I will reduce the amount of pre- and post-shift time necessary to clean up and prepare for tomorrow.
2) I will prepare set up and cleaning checklists and train staff to do some of the work whenever business is slow during the shift.
3) As normal turnover occurs or I replace weak employees, I will make a point of only hiring employees with hustle, allowing fewer employees to handle the workload.
4) I will benchmark customer traffic during shifts to "prove" that we could reduce hours of operation without significantly impacting customer needs or service levels.
5) I will benchmark payroll hours per shift and keep a log of each shift's staffing and my evaluation of service delivery to realistically determine what payroll budget I need next year.

Obstacle: _____

_____

_____

Steps to Overcome: _____

_____

_____

_____

_____

_____

_____

_____

_____

_____

_____

_____

_____

_____

© 2009—Ed Rehkopf

Basics

Learning from Failure

List two of your past failures as a manager.

Example: *We implemented a new expanded wine list in our dining room, but the sales were so disappointing, we pulled it after a month.*

1 _____

2 _____

In hindsight, what might you have done in each of the above situations to achieve a more favorable outcome? Be specific.

Example: <u>I should have been better prepared for the implementation and done a more thorough job of introducing the servers to the new wines. The minimal training I gave was inadequate to the task. Since the servers were unfamiliar with the new offerings, they were in no way prepared to "sell" the new wines.</u>

1 _____

2 _____

MAKING MISTAKES—

"Remember that experience and 'trial and error' can be life's most powerful instructors.

Often the greatest lessons are learned from mistakes. Winning breeds a sense of supremacy and complacency; whereas, losing encourages critical review. Keep this in mind as you blunder along the way."

Leadership on the Line

© 2009—Ed Rehkopf

VALUES—

"Management is doing things right; leadership is doing the right things."

Peter F. Drucker
Author and Management Expert

Leadership on the Line
The Workbook

VALUES—

A leader's values are those bedrock principles that govern the actions by which she gains the trust and loyalty of her followers.

Thoughtfully consider each value in this section. In particular, reflect on how you would respond or react to a boss who lacked such values or whose actions failed to live up to the requirements discussed in this section. Could you trust her? Would you willingly follow her? Would you be able to give your committed and wholehearted efforts to her program or agenda?

Management Professionalism 22
Exercise #1 24
Managers' Code of Ethics 25
Exercise #2 26
Principles of Employee Relations 27
Exercise #3 28

Leadership Values

Notes

Leadership on the Line
The Workbook   Values

MOODS—

"You must set the example and be positive and upbeat. Bad moods can destroy an organization, especially if it is yours. It is your responsibility to keep your employees up. Don't tolerate sour, negative attitudes. Unless you put a stop to them, they will grow like a cancer and be just as destructive.

While you can't control the mood swings of others, you can expect and require your employees to treat their fellow employees with courtesy and respect. You can insist on a cheerful and positive attitude.

Attitudes are clearly infectious and you owe it to others to be as positive and cheerful as possible. One defeatist, grumbling, negative attitude can ruin the day for many others. The sad thing is that you allow the negative person to do this.

So don't tolerate your employees' bad moods. Confront them; shock them back into an acceptable frame of mind. Tell them to go home if they can't be in a better mood. The requirement must be:

'Be of Good Cheer or Don't Be Here!'

Leadership on the Line

© 2009—Ed Rehkopf

Management Professionalism

There are certain fundamental behaviors expected of managers in a business setting. To advance your professional standing and career, adhere to both the spirit and letter of these requirements in all you do.

Consistency in all personnel actions. In today's litigious society, it is essential that all personnel actions from screening interviews, to hiring, to providing opportunities for training and promotion, to counseling, disciplining, and discharging be consistent, fair, and professional.

No retaliation. Employees have a right to come forward with their problems and concerns. While you may expect that they will come to you first, they may feel that you are part of the problem.

Should employees go over your head or file complaints against you, do not retaliate. The best way to avoid this is to have open communications with employees and be approachable for their problems and concerns.

No sexual harassment. Sexual harassment is defined as unwelcome sexual advances, requests for sexual favors, and other verbal or physical conduct of a sexual nature when:

- Submission to such conduct is made either explicitly or implicitly a term or condition of an individual's employment,
- Submission to or rejection of such conduct by an individual is used as the basis for employment decisions affecting the individual, or
- Such conduct has the purpose or the effect of interfering with an individual's work performance or creating an intimidating, hostile, or offensive working environment.

Sexual harassment is against the law and any alleged incident of sexual harassment must be reported to senior management immediately for thorough investigation.

No discriminatory practices. Biases, prejudice, disparaging remarks or jokes on the basis of race, creed, religion, gender, national origin, ethnic group, age, handicap, or sexual orientation cannot be tolerated. There is no place for bigotry or personal and cultural insensitivity in the workplace. While each person may have his or her own biases and prejudices, do not let them interfere with the conduct and performance of your work team.

No favoritism. Scrupulously avoid any appearance of favoritism. The fact or perception of favoritism creates serious problems among employees. Many employee complaints stem from perceptions of unfairness on the part of leaders. Time, money, and energy are spent responding to these complaints. In addition to the problems created for the organization as a whole, the perception of unfairness creates dissension and poor morale and destroys motivation within your work team.

No fraternization with employees. As a leader you must not, under any circumstances, enter into personal, intimate relations with employees under your direction. Should you feel drawn to such a relationship, you must take steps to ensure that one or the other party in the relationship resigns his or her position. Just as nepotism creates problems in an organization, personal relationships can interfere with the performance of your official duties.

(continued)

Leadership on the Line
The Workbook

MAINTAINING PROFESSIONAL DISTANCE—

"The leader can never close the gap between himself and the group. If he does, he is no longer what he must be. He must walk a tightrope between the consent he must win and the control he must exert."

Vince Lombardi
Legendary Green Bay Packer Coach

No fraternization with customers or members. In certain industries, such as private clubs, a leader should avoid fraternization with members beyond the bounds of his job. It is always necessary to have some professional distance from any person or group to whom you have work-related obligations. While you should always treat members with friendliness and courtesy, avoid socializing with them. Such personal relationships may create subtle obligations on your part and will certainly create the appearance of favoritism and/or compromised judgment among other members. These will ultimately lead to resentments and antagonisms, further complicating your already challenging position.

With the exception of club-sponsored events, activities, trips, or the normal socializing as part of the job, invitations from members to private dinners, cocktail parties, card games, and other social activities should be courteously declined. Managers must always remember that they are not members of their clubs, nor do they have equal standing with their members within the context of the club.

No waste, fraud, or abuse. Abide by the highest ethical standards. If you cut corners and bend the rules when it comes to safeguarding the assets of your company, you can expect your employees to do likewise. This is particularly important in regards to your personal productivity. Don't expect your employees to work hard if you don't. Abuse any privilege associated with your position and risk the loss of your employees' respect.

Ethical standards are at the very heart of what you do—your personal and professional integrity. Often the appearance of wrongdoing can be as damaging as the reality. Follow the spirit as well as the letter of ethical requirements and set an unassailable example of conduct for those you lead and serve.

No disclosing confidential information. Never share confidential personnel or disciplinary information. What happens at the workplace should stay there. While it is impossible to control all the rumors and gossip circulating among staff, you can maintain confidentiality and avoid engaging in this activity yourself.

Information about your company, such as financial statements, operating statistics, and internal problems must not be disclosed to persons or organizations external to your business. If a request for information seems legitimate, pass it on to the General Manager who will make the appropriate determination.

No complaining to employees. Leaders shoulder the burden of many responsibilities. When things are not going well, it is all too easy to seek out someone with whom to share the burden. That someone should never be one of your employees.

A major requirement of leaders is to possess the maturity to understand the potential negative consequences of confiding anxieties, doubts, and grievances to subordinates.

No favors from vendors. Frequently, managers will be offered favors and gifts by vendors. These may be in the form of seemingly small personal items, free products for personal use, gifts at holidays or on birthdays, tickets to concerts or sporting events, or invitations to parties to thank you for your patronage. While these may be genuine expressions of appreciation, they create problems for the leader.

Even in subtle ways they cloud your judgment, making it difficult to be truly objective in your purchasing decisions. Accepting even small favors starts you down a slippery path. At what point do you say no, when you have repeatedly said yes?

© 2009—Ed Rehkopf

Values

Exercise #1

Select one of the guidelines from the Management Professionalism list on the previous pages and explain in your own words the reasons for and importance of the guideline, the benefits from following the guideline, and the negative consequences of ignoring it. Consider the reasons not only from your perspective, but also its impact on employee morale and motivation or on customers. The more thorough your explanations, the better your understanding.

Selected guideline: _____

Reasons and Importance: _____

_____

_____

_____

_____

_____

_____

Benefits: _____

_____

_____

_____

_____

_____

_____

_____

Negative Consequences: _____

_____

_____

_____

_____

_____

_____

_____

NEED FOR STRONG LEADERSHIP—

"…without proper training and the inspiring example of leaders above them, young managers, with rare exceptions, will not develop the necessary skills and abilities to become strong leaders. And without strong leadership, any organization will have the same, common set of problems, and will limp along, differentiated only by its own uniquely familiar cast of characters."

Leadership on the Line

© 2009—Ed Rehkopf

Leadership on the Line
The Workbook

Managers' Code of Ethics

1. As a representative of the company for which I work, I understand that my actions and behavior, both at and away from work, reflect on the organization that provides my employment. I will, therefore, do everything in my power to represent them faithfully and professionally in all my dealings with customers, employees, vendors, and the community at large.

2. I will organize the work areas for which I am responsible and thoroughly train the employees I supervise to ensure the most efficient operation with the highest levels of service possible.

3. I will not remove company property for personal use and will protect the company's assets and resources as if they were my own. My vigilance and example will ensure the employees I supervise do likewise.

4. I understand that my leadership and example set the standard for my employees. I understand that a manager who shirks responsibilities, cuts corners, fails to give an honest time commitment, pilfers food and supplies, fails to secure inventories, or is not personally productive in time or commitment, can expect his or her employees to do the same.

5. I will not exchange goods or services for personal favors or services from customers, employees, or vendors. Further, I will not accept personal favors, gifts, or rebates from vendors in any form. Such items benefit me at my employer's expense and are appropriately considered kickbacks. My only interest is to get the best price for my company, and I will make every effort to do so by seeking competitive pricing from several vendors.

6. While I may direct employees' work, their productive effort and well-being serve the interests of the company that employs them. Therefore, I must work hard to ensure their maximum contribution to the mission and goals of the company. I can only do this if I value employees as individuals whose contributions to the collective effort are directly dependent upon my leadership, as well as the tools, training, resources, and support I provide them.

7. I will never use my position or authority to request or require personal services or favors, sexual or otherwise, from employees.

8. I will never enter into personal or intimate relations with any employee who works under my direction or is directly or indirectly supervised by me. Such an inappropriate relationship damages the organization by implications of favoritism and clouded judgment. Ultimately, it irretrievably harms both my ability to lead and my personal and professional reputation.

9. While maintaining a positive interest in and influence over the efforts of my employees, I recognize the importance of maintaining a professional distance from them. I will not socialize or party with those I supervise, except while attending company-sponsored social events or in the furtherance of company business.

10. Finally, I recognize that my integrity is at the core of my personal and professional standing. It is the most important ingredient of my leadership and is the foundation for any success I will achieve in my career and life. I will never be tempted to squander this most precious possession for the sake of expediency or inappropriate gain.

DEFINITION—

Ethics is the discipline dealing with what is good and bad and with moral duty and obligation. It is also a set of moral principles or values and is defined as the principles of conduct governing an individual or a group.

© 2009—Ed Rehkopf

Values

Exercise #2

Select two of the statements from the Managers' Code of Ethics from the previous page and explain in your own words its importance as a quality of leadership.

Example: Selected Principle: *#1*

Our business is located in a small, close-knit community where everybody knows everyone else. One of our supervisors was arrested for a domestic disturbance and it was reported in the local newspaper. Though he was a strong manager, respected by both customers and employees, the resulting embarrassment for the company led the owners to discharge him. They felt that his actions set a poor example for his employees, damaged his ability to lead effectively, and were offensive to customers and the community at large.

Selected Principle: ___

_____
_____
_____
_____
_____
_____
_____
_____

Selected Principle: ___

_____
_____
_____
_____
_____
_____
_____
_____

ETHICS—

"The supreme quality for leadership is unquestionably integrity. Without it, no real success is possible, no matter whether it is on a section gang, a football field, in an army, or in an office."

Dwight D. Eisenhower
U.S. President

© 2009—Ed Rehkopf

Leadership on the Line
The Workbook

VALUE YOUR PEOPLE—

"We acknowledge each operation as a team of dedicated individuals working toward common goals and we recognize the ultimate value of people in everything we do."

Leadership on the Line

© 2009—Ed Rehkopf

Principles of Employee Relations

It is a leader's intention to create and sustain a work environment that promotes happy and satisfied employees, thereby ensuring positive customer experiences. Therefore:

1. All employees will be treated with dignity, courtesy, and respect.

2. Pledge to conduct employee relations in an honest and straightforward way. Any necessary criticism or counseling will be conducted in private in a constructive manner with the intention of instructing and correcting rather than blaming.

3. Every employee contributes to the overall success of the operation. The only difference among employees is their level of authority and responsibility. Every employee is important.

4. The great majority of people want to do their jobs well and take pride in their work. When an employee fails, it is often a failure of management to properly train or communicate performance expectations. In other words, you can't expect employees to do something properly unless you have properly shown them how to do it.

5. Employees have no idea what goals management has for them unless those goals are communicated. They have a need and the right to know how their performance is contributing to the achievement of those goals. Continuous feedback is essential.

6. Management must make every practical effort to keep employees informed on matters concerning standards, policies, procedures, long range plans, projects, work conditions, and compensation and benefits. An informed employee is a better employee. Supervisors should be available at reasonable times to answer questions and hear employee concerns.

7. Recognition is important to everyone. If you have the authority to correct, you also have the responsibility to praise. You cannot have one without the other.

8. Everyone has a responsibility to help fellow employees. We do not work alone. Rather we work together for a common purpose. We owe it to ourselves and everyone we work with to be personally pleasant and mutually supportive. One unpleasant personality or negative, non-cooperative attitude can ruin the workplace for all of us.

9. Empower your employees through meaningful contribution, while striving to make the workplace interesting, challenging, and rewarding. You can do this by involving employees in decision-making and continual process improvement. The willing, committed, and empowered involvement of your employees is truly the driving force behind any success you may achieve as an organization.

10. The workplace must also be pleasant, enjoyable, and even fun. Too much of our lives are given to work for it to be viewed as a necessary drudgery. Each employee should be challenged to do everything possible within good taste and reason to make their workplace more enjoyable for all.

Values

Exercise #3

Select two of the Principles of Employee Relations from the previous page and explain in your own words its importance to building a strong relationship between the leader and her followers.

Example: Selected Principle: *#1*

If a leader doesn't have a genuine respect for each employee's dignity and worth, she will consciously or unconsciously denigrate the person. This will create resentment on the part of the employee who, in turn, will not be able to wholeheartedly support the efforts and agenda of the leader. In addition, other employees may pick up on the leader's treatment of the employee and follow the bad example she sets.

Selected Principle: ___

_____
_____
_____
_____
_____
_____
_____
_____

Selected Principle: ___

_____
_____
_____
_____
_____
_____
_____
_____

YOUR TEAM—

"As a group of people committed to common goals, you can only achieve your team's greatest potential by taking advantage of the talent, initiative, and ingenuity of each and every one of your employees. To the extent that any individual is not valued, trained, and motivated, your enterprise suffers."

Leadership on the Line

© 2009—Ed Rehkopf

LEADERSHIP—

"If you want to be a leader, you have to have followers."

Colin Powell
U.S. Secretary of State, Chairman of the Joint Chiefs of Staff

Leadership on the Line
The Workbook

LESSONS—

This section contains a number of leadership lessons that reinforce or augment the material found in *Leadership on the Line*.

As you read each lesson, attempt to connect the topics covered to your own experiences and consider how you might modify your leadership approach for better results.

Authority, Responsibility, Accountability 32
Relationships 33
Charisma and Trust 34
Consistency and Common Decency 35
Exercise #4 36
Active and Engaged Leadership 37
Our Need to Serve 39
The Hierarchy of Service 40
Ego-Driven Failure 42
Leadership Growth and Adaptation 43
Projecting Confidence 44
Personal Responsibility 45
Leadership and a Failure of Engagement 46
Exercise #5 47
Morale Matters 48
Do the Right Thing 49
Value Your People 51

Leadership Lessons

Notes

Leadership on the Line
The Workbook   Lessons

Authority, Responsibility, Accountability

"Authority," "Responsibility," and "Accountability" are three terms that are used frequently in connection with positions of leadership. What exactly do these terms mean and how are they related?

Authority is defined as "a power or right, delegated or given." In this sense, **the person or company that hires a leader vests him with the authority to manage or direct a particular operation.** It is expected that this individual will exercise the full scope of his authority to properly, profitably, and professionally manage the operation.

Responsibility is defined as "a particular burden of obligation upon a person who is responsible." Responsible is defined as "answerable or accountable, as for something within one's power or control." Therefore, **a leader is responsible and has responsibility for the operation for which she has been given authority.**

Accountability is defined as "subject to the obligation to report, explain, or justify something; answerable." **A leader is answerable for the performance of the operation for which he has authority and is responsible.**

Authority may be delegated to subordinates. For example, a general manager may delegate the authority to collect delinquent accounts to the controller. The controller then has the right to perform tasks associated with collection, such as sending past due notices, charging finance charges on delinquent accounts, and recommending bad debt write-off for seriously overdue accounts. However, even though the general manager delegated the authority, he or she still has the responsibility to ensure that collections are done properly. As the saying goes, **"You can delegate authority, but not responsibility."** Even when you delegate, you are ultimately responsible for your organization's performance.

As a leader, you are accountable for those functions and tasks that have been delegated to you. Likewise, should you delegate any functions or tasks to subordinates, you must ensure that they are held accountable for properly performing them. This requires that you properly explain your expectations to subordinates.

This is most easily done when performance parameters are objective, say telling an advertising executive she must retain her major accounts or else she'll be replaced. More often, performance parameters are more complex and involve subjective evaluations. Regardless of the difficulties in defining these parameters, it must be done. Otherwise, there is no way to hold a subordinate accountable for results. It is for this reason that performance standards must be defined. Often, detailed benchmarks, consistently and conscientiously tracked over time, will provide the most meaningful measures of performance.

AUTHORITY, RESPONSIBILITY, AND ACCOUNTABILITY—

"Too often we expect people to be loyal to the position of a leader instead of the person who occupies that position. But people are not motivated by organizational charts; they respond to people. The first thing a leader must declare is not authority because of rights, but authority because of relationships. People do not care how much you know until they know how much you care. You've got to give loyalty down before you receive loyalty up. If people do not believe in their leader, anything will hinder them from following. If people believe in their leader, nothing will stop them."

John C. Maxwell
Developing the Leader Within You

© 2009—Ed Rehkopf

Leadership on the Line
The Workbook

Relationships

John C. Maxwell, author of the bestselling *The 21 Irrefutable Laws of Leadership*, says that the definition of leadership is **influence**. While it is, first and foremost, the ability to influence followers, it also requires that the leader influence those people who make up any and all constituencies.

In a free society, all but the most economically disadvantaged have choices—they can choose to work for you and your business or they can take their talents and abilities elsewhere. It is, therefore, the manner in which you as a leader engage them that determines your level of influence.

Influence is derived from the relationships you create with your followers and other constituents. How you act and interact with others is the basis for your success as a leader. **The quality of your relationships will determine your outcomes**. But you must understand that each of your followers and constituents is a unique individual with different needs and motivations. What may work with one may fail miserably with another. And, unfortunately, creating meaningful relationships with other people can be a great challenge for all of us—witness all the dysfunctional families, rocky romances, and failed marriages—and no less challenging for leaders who must interact with a wide variety of followers.

But the art of relationships can be learned. Generally speaking, while it requires experience, judgment, a measure of sensitivity to the needs of others, and a fair degree of emotional maturity, the ability to form and sustain meaningful relationships improves with age.

Developing leadership, or relationship skills, is a cumulative process. It's why Jim Collins, author of *Good to Great, Why Some Companies Make the Leap . . . and Others Don't*, proposes the Level 5 Hierarchy leading to the consummate Level 5 Leader. It is why potential leaders must be identified early, why young managers must be trained in the skills of leadership, and why such skills should be nurtured and shaped with each increase in responsibility and each step of the career ladder. Clearly, the rudimentary skills of direct face-to-face leadership that serve the front line supervisor so well are inadequate for the more complex and subtle exercise of authority required of a mid-level manager or senior executive.

Creating and sustaining meaningful relationships is at the heart of Service-Based Leadership. The extent to which you are able to develop those relationships early in your career will have a great bearing on your future success—but not only in your career. The bonus is that in developing Service-Based Leadership skills, you develop the skills to form meaningful relationships in other areas of your life.

RELATIONSHIPS—

"People who are unable to build solid, lasting relationships will soon discover that they are unable to sustain long, effective leadership."

John C. Maxwell
Developing the Leader Within You

© 2009—Ed Rehkopf

Lessons

Charisma and Trust

People often speak of an especially effective leader's charisma—that somewhat mysterious ability to connect with people in a profound and moving way. We can all think of leaders, usually on the national or international stage, who possessed charisma. Some names that come to mind include Eleanor Roosevelt, with her quick wit and commitment to social equity, Ronald Reagan, called the "Great Communicator" for his skill in connecting with people, and Martin Luther King, Jr., for his soaring oratory and message of non-violent change and justice. More recently we recognize Oprah Winfrey for her engaging manner and willingness to raise awareness of a multitude of issues affecting people's lives.

While charisma can add to a leader's skill set, it must be based upon a foundation of trust. Without earned and merited trust, a charismatic personality is little more than a con artist.

Two important ways to gain and hold the trust of followers and other constituents is to demonstrate both **integrity** and **competence** in all you do.

Integrity is not simply honesty, though truth and truthfulness are significant parts of it. Ultimately integrity is being true to yourself and your beliefs. The dictionary defines integrity as "the adherence to moral or ethical principles." This implies that one's actions match her words—that she does what she says she will do regardless of consequences, that she has a moral compass that guides her in all instances, that she can be counted on to do the right thing. At the end of the day, a person who has integrity can be trusted by others in all situations.

In addition to possessing integrity a leader must demonstrate competence. No one wants to follow someone who is inept, no matter what authority he may possess. In fighting wars a follower's life may depend upon it. During the Civil War a fellow officer said of Gen. Nathaniel Banks that it was murder to send soldiers out under him. While this political appointee of President Lincoln had the authority to command, he clearly did not possess the competence to lead.

The U.S. Marine Corps in its Fundamentals of Marine Corps Leadership tells its aspiring leaders that they must be technically and tactically proficient. To develop this ability, they are told to "seek a well-rounded [professional] education" and to "seek out and associate with capable leaders. [To] observe and study their actions." Lastly, Marines are told to prepare themselves for the job of leader at the next higher rank. This advice applies to leadership in any situation or endeavor.

By cultivating and demonstrating both integrity and competence in all you do, you will gain the trust of your followers. While only a gifted few possess natural charisma, it may be argued that it is not required for the smaller arenas in which most of us labor. Yet as you continue to grow and nurture your leadership skills through practice and experience, you may discover that your followers consider your leadership to be charismatic. As with beauty, charisma is in the eye of the beholder.

CHARISMA—

The dictionary offers three definitions of charisma:

"Theological: a divinely conferred gift or power."

"The special quality that gives an individual influence or authority over large numbers of people."

"The special virtue of an office, position, etc., that confers, or is thought to confer, on the person holding it an unusual ability for leadership, worthiness of veneration, or the like."

The Random House College Dictionary

© 2009—Ed Rehkopf

Leadership on the Line
The Workbook

Consistency and Common Decency

In addition to possessing integrity and demonstrating competence, leaders must also be consistent in their values and vision. Such **consistency** requires a foundation of principles for one's actions and a well-developed guide for how to proceed. Followers will quickly lose confidence in an erratic leader or one without a clear and compelling vision.

Being consistent does not in any way imply rigidity or inflexibility in your thinking, planning, or execution. A hallmark of leadership is the recognition that we operate in a fluid world where everything changes all the time. As German military theorist von Moltke said, "No battle plan survives contact with the enemy." The same could be said for any plan and the constantly unfolding realities faced by every enterprise.

When a leader demonstrates consistent values and a persistent pursuit of well-defined objectives, followers can feel confident in their leader and the direction he is taking them. An unpredictable leader, who bounces from one initiative to another and whose plans, performance, and behavior are constantly changing, creates a situation much like the Doom Loop described by Jim Collins in *Good to Great*.

> "The comparison companies followed a different pattern, the doom loop. Rather than accumulating momentum – turn by turn of the flywheel – they tried to skip buildup and jump immediately to breakthrough. Then, with disappointing results, they'd lurch back and forth, failing to maintain consistent direction."

Employees can deal with some agenda changes from senior management, but continually changing initiatives sap them of their enthusiasm and willingness to adapt. This is particularly so when they are not involved in decision-making and they are not treated as if they matter.

This brings us to **common decency** and how followers are treated. While every person may have his or her own conception of what is decent, common decency encompasses those behaviors considered to be the ideal in human intercourse. Among them are:

- Respect—regard or consideration for others and their needs.
- Sensitivity—heightened awareness to needs and concerns of others.
- Courtesy—polite behavior, respect, consideration, helpfulness.
- Kindness—goodwill, generosity, charity, and sympathy toward others.
- Generosity of Spirit—absence of meanness or smallness of mind or character.

When a leader demonstrates these behaviors in his dealings with all constituents, it naturally creates strong, trusting relationships. Once again, though, consistency is essential. A leader cannot be kind one day and callous the next and expect his constituents to trust him.

As children we are taught the common decency of the Golden Rule—treating others as we wish to be treated. But as we grow older we are often faced with stressful situations and unpleasant people who cause us to develop our own defensive responses and disagreeable behaviors.

Yet, just as these habits were learned over time, they can be unlearned by conscious effort. While we cannot control what happens to us, we can control our reactions to events. Making the effort to treat others well will go a long way toward building meaningful relationships with all constituents.

PERSONAL NOTE—

Many years ago while visiting the beach for a weekend getaway I found a book entitled *Try Giving Yourself Away* on a shelf in a motel lobby. This easy-to-read book first published in 1947 had a profound impact on me. I recommend it to anyone who would like a simple, effective, and fun way to help change the way you view and interact with others. See the bibliography at the end of *The Workbook* for more information.

© 2009—Ed Rehkopf

Lessons

THE BASIS OF TRUST—

Trust is the most important ingredient of leadership. In our society where employees have a choice about where they work, the best employees, the ones you work so hard to attract, hire, and retain, have many employment options. Why would they want to work for a bad boss, for someone who does not respect them, treat them well, support them, or provide them with meaningful and satisfying employment? Why would they continue to work for someone they can't trust to do the right things?

Gaining the trust of your followers, then, is the most critical thing you can do to win their willing and committed support.

Exercise #4

Think about the important relationships in your life—your spouse or significant other, your parents and relatives, your best friends, your co-workers and acquaintances, and the people you want to spend time with. How important is it for you to trust these people and what is it that allows you to trust them? List two important relationships in your life and explain what it is that allows you to have complete confidence and trust in that person.

Example: *My brother*

He is two years older than me and all my life he has looked out for me and guided me through my tough times. He taught me to play sports and always included me in his circle of friends. He is honest and straightforward. I can always count on him to do the right thing. We have always shared our deepest concerns and he has never broken that confidence. He listens to me when I have problems and helps out in any way he can. He always has my best interests at heart. He has never let me down.

1. _____

2. _____

© 2009—Ed Rehkopf

Leadership on the Line
The Workbook

ADVANCING YOUR CAREER—

"If you are interested in advancing your career, the easiest and quickest way to do so is to add value to your employer. When you consistently demonstrate your ability to take initiative, solve problems, and make your boss' job easier, you will be recognized as one who adds value to the organization. The principles embodied in the concept of "Active and Engaged Leadership" will allow you to stand head and shoulders above your peers and will ultimately lead to greater and greater successes in life."

Leadership on the Line

Active and Engaged Leadership

Reject the Status Quo. Every organization has its way of doing things. Often its methods are a result of stopgap measures implemented over time to quickly deal with various problems. Seldom are policies and procedures formalized in writing, and even less often are they well-thought out from a big picture standpoint. Despite the haphazard nature of most methods, they are considered sacred and untouchable by employees because "we've always done it that way."

An Active and Engaged Leader, however, does not accept this status quo. He or she shines the fresh light of reason on the organization, continually asking questions—Is there a better way to do this? Does this make sense? Does this really serve our customers' interests? Can I do this more efficiently another way?

This willingness to look for new ways to do things allows the Active and Engaged Leader to realize the next principle . . .

Seek Continual Improvement. Every aspect of an operation—from product and services to standards, policies, procedures, work methods, and training material—should be analyzed for ways to do them better, more efficiently, and with higher levels of service.

When a leader is dedicated to continual improvement and seeks the input of his empowered employees, the entire department becomes energized with ideas, innovation, and enthusiasm. And while the company as a whole and its customers benefit from the improvements, the employees gain the greatest benefit—knowing that their efforts contribute in a meaningful way to the success of the organization.

Be Proactive. A leader should also be looking ahead to ensure her department is ready for any contingency. While most businesses have a seasonal routine, the Active and Engaged Leader reviews past activity for ways to improve and continually seeks new ideas, events, and activities to keep the enterprise interesting and fresh for its customers and employees.

Managers should always be looking at least three months out for routine operations, and further for major activities, events, or projects. This continually advancing planning horizon allows all planning requirements to be completed in a timely manner and allows sufficient time to order supplies and materials, put advance notice in newsletters or marketing pieces, and prepare appropriate staffing schedules.

Have a Plan. Every event, activity, project, or initiative demands a plan. Without a proper plan you approach everything helter-skelter, waste valuable resources and time, and subject your employees to your own disorganization and lack of discipline.

By putting your plan in writing—even as simple as a one page outline of timing and responsibilities—you are better able to communicate your plan to your employees and to other affected departments. Such a written plan also broadcasts your competence and abilities to everyone who sees it.

The Army had a phrase to express the need for planning. The sanitized version of the six P's is:

"Prior Planning Prevents P...-Poor Performance"

© 2009—Ed Rehkopf

(continued)

Lessons

Follow-Through and Follow-Up. Whatever she undertakes, the Active and Engaged Leader will follow through to ensure that all details are covered and all actions completed. Often follow-through requires adjustments to the original plan when unexpected situations arise.

Lastly, the Active and Engaged Leader will follow up on all completed actions or projects to learn from mistakes and to ensure that the initiative met the expectations of customers, other managers, and employees.

Summary. Being an Active and Engaged Leader is more of a mindset than possessing specific skills. It involves the willingness to tackle any problem, the understanding that every problem has a solution, and the realization that problems are opportunities that come knocking.

The choice to be an Active and Engaged Leader or one who only "reacts" to events is up to you. On the one hand, you'll add value to your organization and ensure your future success; on the other, you'll tread water and wonder why your career isn't going anywhere.

Reflection: Select one of the principles of Active and Engaged Leadership and discuss what steps you might take to add value to your organization in your current position. Consider a recent or current problematic situation or opportunity. Be specific about those things you might do.

MAGNIFY YOUR IMPACT—

"To the extent that your leadership efforts are based on service to others rather than your personal ambitions, your success will be magnified. Employees will more willingly dedicate themselves to any endeavor when part of a team effort and when they feel that their interests are also being served."

Leadership on the Line

© 2009—Ed Rehkopf

Leadership on the Line
The Workbook

THE FLYWHEEL EFFECT—

"Stop and think about it for a minute. What do the right people want more than anything else? They want to be part of a winning team. They want to contribute to producing visible, tangible results. They want to feel the excitement of being involved in something that just flat-out works. When the right people see a simple plan born of confronting the brutal facts—a plan developed from understanding, not bravado—they are likely to say, 'That'll work. Count me in.' When they see the monolithic unity of the executive team behind the simple plan and the selfless, dedicated qualities of Level 5 leadership, they'll drop their cynicism. When people begin to feel the magic of momentum—when they begin to see tangible results, when they can feel the flywheel beginning to build speed—that's when the bulk of people line up to throw their shoulders against the wheel and push."

        Jim Collins
        Good to Great, Why Some Companies Make the Leap … and Others Don't

© 2009—Ed Rehkopf

Our Need to Serve

Jim Collins says that people "want to be involved in something that just flat-out works," but I believe it is something more. I believe that people have a great need to connect with or serve something larger than themselves. Whether it's building a skyscraper, embarking on a campaign to eradicate hunger, working on the design of an award-winning advertising campaign, or even dressing in favorite NFL team colors and attending all the home games—people need to connect to a larger purpose or endeavor.

Great leaders understand this basic human need and have the ability to create that connection for their followers; unfortunately, not always to good purpose—witness Hitler's rise to power and spell-binding hold on the German people or, in recent times, the illusion of success created by the leaders of ENRON before its financial collapse.

But the connection I am talking about need not be a life-altering cause or event. Most of us live rather uneventful lives. While our need is to earn a living and support our families, an astute leader recognizes the opportunity to create something out-of-the-ordinary—a special enterprise that performs better than others and is a source of purpose and pride for all.

In connecting people to the challenge of creating something special, the leader feeds the employees' need to do something beyond self while advancing the purpose of the enterprise. All that is necessary is for the leader to frame the challenge in terms of shared goals. In the service industry this is a fairly simple task. **Our purpose is to serve**. The quality of our service encourages customers and repeat business, which in turn ensures the success of the enterprise for the owners, and, ultimately, the job security and advancement opportunities of everyone involved.

Throughout my career, I have met many eager, enthusiastic young people, some just starting out their adult lives and relishing the opportunity of their first jobs. Unfortunately for most, their youthful idealism is crushed pretty quickly by the realities of the workplace, particularly when they are not well-led, when they are not properly trained or supported, and when they are treated as if they didn't matter.

At the same time, I've heard managers complain about the poor state of the labor pool and their inability to find decent employees who have commitment to their jobs. Listening to such complaints I have to wonder what steps these individuals have taken to motivate their employees, to provide training and meaningful work experiences, to connect their workers' labors to a larger effort.

To expect that the wide variety of applicants for positions will inherently know and understand a leader's vision and the values that underlie the enterprise's efforts is foolish. All employees, whether first-time job seekers or those who have worked in a variety of jobs and settings, need the vision of connecting to a larger purpose, and they need a Service-Based Leader who can provide them the meaningful employment that serves their greater needs.

Lessons

The Hierarchy of Service

While *Leadership on the Line* stresses that the leader must serve the needs of his or her constituencies, not all constituent needs have equal weight or importance.

Owners or shareholders are usually the smallest constituent group in numbers, but their needs are paramount. Why? Because it is their capital that has been invested in the enterprise and their need for return on investment that permits the continuation of the business. If it is not making a profit, if it cannot gain credit based on a potential for future profit, if it cannot meet its cash needs for payroll or to pay vendors, it will quickly go out of business and the needs of all other constituencies will become irrelevant.

Obviously, a return on investment is important. Consider why an owner would want to earn 2% in a business when he could invest his money in a less risky venture and earn a better return. While there may be other reasons for continuing to own a business—such as prestige; a sense of obligation to family, community, or employees; or the expectation of improved future performance—over the long haul owners will not be willing to risk their capital on a poor-performing venture.

The basis for the traditional hierarchical organizational model is the military concept of "chain of command." In this model, management is represented as the sequence of authority in executing the will of the owners—and certainly management plays that essential role. But in addition to not representing the importance of customers, it also places the employees at the bottom of the chain—thereby visually relegating them to the position of least consequence.

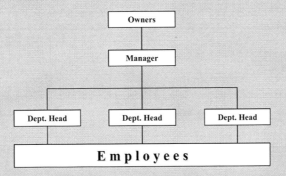

Traditional Top-Down Organizational Chart

It properly emphasizes the place of owners, but where are the customers?

Next in order of importance are the needs of **customers.** Without sufficient customers patronizing the business, it will not be profitable or viable. If not viable, it will not last long—and all constituencies lose.

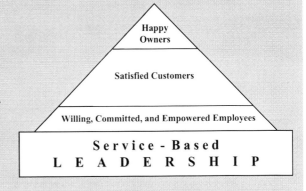

Service-Based Organizational Model

Here the importance of satisfying customers is depicted, as is the important role of employees. The organization's leaders are placed at the bottom, clearly emphasizing their role in serving the needs of all constituencies.

(continued)

THE PYRAMID OF SUCCESSFUL SERVICE—

"To the extent that you make your employees a part of your efforts, teach them, and share your goals and challenges with them, they will become willing and committed helpers in your quest for quality and service.

Imagine the benefit of ten people trying to meet goals and budgets instead of one. Think of the natural enthusiasm that can be mustered when your benchmarks become theirs. Recognize the pride of accomplishment they will feel when the team not only meets, but exceeds expectations. This is truly a formula for success.

In simplest terms, when you serve your employees, they will serve your customers, who by their continued enthusiastic patronage will serve the needs of your shareholders."

Leadership on the Line

© 2009—Ed Rehkopf

Leadership on the Line
The Workbook

Ultimately, customers are attracted by price and the quality of products and services. Taken together, quality and price create a sense of value—the value perceived by customers. If enough customers perceive value, they will frequent the enterprise to spend their money and will make it successful. If not, the business will ultimately fail.

This statement brings us to our third constituency—the **employees**. They are the ones who execute the owners' vision for quality of product and service. They are the ones whose daily interaction with customers creates the value customers seek. Properly led, valued, and supported, employees will enthusiastically commit to serving the business' customers thereby fostering levels of business that enable it to thrive.

Reflection: *The book, Leadership on the Line, and this Workbook both stress the importance of Service-Based Leadership.*

Explain the term "service" and what it means to be a Service-Based Leader.

_____
_____
_____
_____
_____
_____
_____

List some of the things you can do to better serve your employees.

_____
_____
_____
_____
_____
_____
_____

Why does Service-Based Leadership place so much emphasis on serving the needs of your employees?

_____
_____
_____
_____
_____
_____

WHO GUARANTEES YOUR JOB?

"I can't guarantee you a job and a union steward can't guarantee you a job, only a customer can."

Michael Hammer
Business Consultant

© 2009—Ed Rehkopf

Lessons

Ego-Driven Failure

As quoted in the sidebar, Jim Collins says his research showed that gargantuan personal egos do not lead to corporate success. In wondering why, here are a few observations:

Ego-centric individuals are all about themselves. As such they have difficulty creating the relationships with followers that sustain the efforts of an organization. While they may drive results by their force of will in the short-term, they often create resentments and divisions that harm the organization over the long haul.

Ego-centric leaders think they have all the answers which make it hard for them to listen to other opinions or to become educated beyond their own pre-conceived notions. A lack of understanding of the true situation drastically hampers their chance for success.

Ego-centric people tend to attract and retain "Yes Men" while driving away "A" Players. Strong subordinates expect to participate and be heard and will not long stay in a job where they are not given an opportunity to participate in decisions or make a difference. As pointed out in *Good to Great*, when the ego-centric leader departs, there is not a strong successor waiting in the wings or any depth of talent in the senior management ranks.

Ego-centric leaders want all the credit for success and are more likely to blame others for failures. Followers are quick to grasp this selfish behavior and have little respect for or desire to support such a leader. Without the willing involvement of followers no endeavor will succeed for long.

Ego-centric people want to be star players and do not build teams. In this modern age, worthwhile enterprises and endeavors are far too complex for any one person to completely grasp. Success can only come by assembling a team of talented individuals who understand all the relevant disciplines and can implement them effectively.

Ego-centric leaders are incapable of empowering others. It's just not part of their makeup to care enough about others to make the effort on their behalf. Without empowered employees at all levels of the organization, problems will abound.

While an ego-driven leader can achieve spectacular success by force of will and personality, he will never become a "great" leader as suggested by Andrew Carnegie, and will never "build the enduring greatness" of a Level 5 leader as posited by Jim Collins.

IMPACT OF EGO—

"Level 5 leaders display a compelling modesty, are self-effacing and understated. In contrast, two thirds of the comparison companies had leaders with gargantuan personal egos that contributed to the demise or continued mediocrity of the company."

Jim Collins
Good to Great, Why Some Companies Make the Leap …and Others Don't

"No man will make a great leader who wants to do it all himself, or to get all the credit for doing it."

Andrew Carnegie
Industrialist and Philanthropist

© 2009—Ed Rehkopf

Leadership on the Line
The Workbook

TYPES OF LEADERSHIP—

"Since there are many types of leaders—political, intellectual, military, industrial, business, financial, athletic, and so on for any conceivable endeavor and profession—the skills and abilities that might make a person successful in one arena do not necessarily guarantee success in another.

Many people hold positions of authority by virtue of ownership, heredity, education, oratorical skill, appointment, election, circumstances, or even bluff, but the exercise of authority doesn't necessarily make them leaders. The position of President, CEO, General, Doctor, or Professor may command respect, deference, even fear, but they do not necessarily have the willing commitment and loyalty of their followers unless this has been earned by the exercise of leadership."

Leadership on the Line

© 2009—Ed Rehkopf

Leadership Growth and Adaptation

As any individual grows in leadership, his ideas about what leadership entails will mature and, in that maturation, one constant will stand out—change. Adaptation to insistently changing circumstances is a hallmark of success. One must approach life as a continual learning experience.

What attitudes and approaches lend themselves to this continual learning experience?

1. Always keep an open mind. Try not to pre-judge situations or people.
2. Never assume you know it all. The more you learn, the more you realize how little you know.
3. Be open and accessible to constituents—particularly followers.
4. Remember that each follower and each constituent is unique and may require different motivators.
5. Take time to stop and listen to your constituents. In your rush to accomplish, do not forget that you need their input, feedback, and support. Knowing their needs is essential.
6. Don't cast others as adversaries. Find out their legitimate concerns about your agenda. Accept the challenge of winning over your most difficult constituents.
7. Take constituent concerns seriously and adjust your agenda as necessary. Their buy-in to your program is essential to your success. Judicious compromise is a sign of intelligence and flexibility, not defeat. It should never be "my way or the highway."
8. Stay informed. Know what's going on in your organization, community, and the world at large. To be effective, you must be relevant to your time and place. To speak with authority and win people over, you must be knowledgeable about more than just your job.
9. Nurture and care for your constituents. While never on a *quid pro quo* basis, you will find that the care you give will be returned many times over in loyalty, support, and advancement of your goals.
10. Be aware and alert to what goes on around you. Learn by observing others, by witnessing their successes and failures. Most knowledge comes not from education, but from your life experiences. When you go through life in a fog of your own making—too consumed with real and imaginary dramas—you are inert, like a rock, to the wealth of learning opportunities around you. As one leading hospitality company puts it, "keep your antennas up and your radar on" at all times—you'll learn a lot by doing so!
11. When you're stressed or something has you ill-at-ease or on edge, it is a sure sign that something is wrong somewhere. Analyze your situation. Discovering the source is the first step in finding out what's wrong and where you need to act.
12. Once you've discovered the problem, contemplate how your leadership can overcome the issue. Like any other learned ability, this continual "puzzling" over leadership challenges will enhance your skills and usually bring you to a better resolution. If things turn out badly, figure out what went wrong and learn from the mistake.

Darwin was right on many levels when he said that creatures have to adapt to survive. Leaders must adapt, not just to survive, but to thrive.

Lessons

Projecting Confidence

We all have varying degrees of self-confidence. What creates a self-confident person is something of a mystery—maybe upbringing, education, or some deeper subconscious quality. Most of us are self-confident about those things we know well or have experience with and less sure when we are on new ground. There are managers who mask their inadequacies and insecurities with arrogance and bluff, but it is pretty obvious by their lack of production and performance that this is just a façade to hide their shortcomings.

Given that young managers are often short on experience, it is understandable that they may lack confidence in much that they are called on to do. While each leader must recognize and cope with his or her own levels of self-confidence, it's absolutely necessary that a leader project confidence in all he or she attempts to do. Followers want to believe in their leaders and any faltering of will or perceived lack of confidence will undermine their commitment to the task at hand.

So how does one project confidence, even when beset by doubt? The following can help even the most unsure leader appear more confident. And keep in mind that as you progress through your career your accumulating experience will build your self-confidence.

Recognize the importance of projecting self-confidence. Consider the impact on followers when their leader acts and performs like "a deer in headlights."

Think ahead and prepare. Many world-class athletes visualize their performance in advance to achieve better results. Leaders should do the same. The more you think ahead and prepare for those occasions when your leadership is on display, the more comfortable you'll be in any situation. The more comfortable you are, the more confident you'll be. When you are organized and efficient, you naturally exude an air of competence and confidence. When you are chaotic and confused, you scare the heck out of your followers and undermine their confidence in you.

Take stock of your weaknesses. Knowing where you are weak will help you develop a plan to work on strengthening those areas.

Play to your strengths. Organize situations to play to your strengths. The more positive leadership experiences you have, the more "strengths" and confidence you'll possess.

Be aware of and learn from the leadership examples of others. For good or bad, you can learn a lot by observing others—your superiors and peers. Analyze successful leadership techniques and ask yourself what could be done to improve upon or avoid instances of poor leadership.

Keep your cool. The essence of good leadership is not losing your head when things are going badly. It is at these times when your followers need your steady hand and guidance more than ever.

It is possible, even when filled with doubt, to project an air of confidence. Doing so will inspire your followers. Not doing so will fill them with doubt about the endeavor and their leader.

CONFIDENCE—

"The very essence of leadership is that you have to have vision. You can't blow an uncertain trumpet."

Theodore M. Hesburgh
President Emeritus
Notre Dame University

© 2009—Ed Rehkopf

Leadership on the Line
The Workbook

RESPONSIBILITY—

"Success on any major scale requires you to accept responsibility.... In the final analysis, the one quality that all successful people have is the ability to take on responsibility."

Michael Korda
*Editor-in-Chief,
Simon & Schuster*

"Ninety-nine percent of all failures come from people who have a habit of making excuses."

George Washington Carver
*American Scientist,
Inventor and Educator*

© 2009—Ed Rehkopf

Personal Responsibility

Soldiers are drilled repeatedly that the proper answer for any questioned failure is "No excuse, Sir!" While this response seems to be a martinet-like reply when being chewed out for poorly-shined shoes, an unpolished belt buckle, or for failing to accomplish some impossible task, the underlying message is an important one—**that there is no excuse for failure.**

Properly understood it means that there is always more that you, as a leader, could have done to succeed—you could have paid closer attention, devoted more resources, better juggled the demands on your time and attention, done a better job of planning or preparing, selected better teammates or subordinates, delegated more or better, supervised closer, or any other more appropriate action or initiative that would have ensured success.

The concept of no excuse for failure is an important one in fighting wars, winning football games, running companies, or any other worthwhile endeavor. Further, the concept of no excuses implies that you cannot blame others for your failure—**there is always something more you could have done.**

While the concept of personal responsibility may seem overwhelming in its implications, it is in fact the ultimate expression of empowerment. It should not be understood as "It's always my bad," but instead as "I can fix it, solve it, repair it." By accepting this level of personal responsibility you can negotiate your way to success in any endeavor by choosing to make it so.

Another lesson the military teaches is that **a leader is responsible for everything his unit does or fails to do.** While this lesson is closely tied to "no excuse for failure," it brings some important distinctions with it—that no matter what role others are supposed to play in the endeavor—**it is the leader who is ultimately responsible for the outcome.**

Some examples to illustrate the point: Too often, managers wash their hands of personnel issues because they have a human resource department. The same is true when the company has a training department or is provided with training materials. Suddenly, the manager is no longer responsible for the training outcome because "someone else has that covered." Such attitudes set the manager up for failure.

Remembering that **"you can delegate authority, but not responsibility,"** the manager must take personal responsibility to ensure that not only is she knowledgeable about HR issues and labor laws, but that all subordinate managers are as well. Likewise, the manager must be intimately familiar with training materials and whether subordinate managers are properly training front-line employees. To do otherwise is to avoid the very responsibilities for which she was hired.

While these leadership lessons from the military may seem overly stringent, even harsh, they are, in fact, the essence of leadership—**taking personal responsibility**.

Lessons

Leadership and a Failure of Engagement

Most leaders readily understand the negative impact of a hostile work environment on employees. Employees who aren't properly trained, who aren't given the tools and resources to do their jobs, and who are demeaned by the abusive actions of supervisors or other employees, cannot contribute effectively to the team effort and the success of their organization.

A more subtle factor in creating a hostile work environment is the supervisor who does not engage with his team or who doesn't pay attention to what is going on in his section or department. Consider that:

- Individuals in any group setting rarely have neutral feelings toward or about the others in the group. They like some and dislike others, usually for their own, sometimes hard to discern, reasons.
- People are naturally attracted to and spend time with those they like and avoid those they don't. This results in cliques of the included and, outside the cliques, the excluded.
- The excluded often feel jealous, resentful, and fearful because of their exclusion.
- In the absence of ongoing timely and accurate information, fearful people assume the worst. Fearful people can be paranoid and perceive discrimination, favoritism, and abuse where none may exist.
- A fragmented work team cannot perform effectively.

When a supervisor does not engage daily with team members, give specific directions regarding work assignments, and communicate thoroughly about all matters affecting the team, the fragmented team will gossip, backbite, and bicker among themselves.

Seldom will they work together effectively and often their antagonisms affect customers and co-workers. Sometimes their behavior is passive-aggressive—trying to sabotage the efforts of others, all the while acting helpful and friendly.

If all this seems outlandish or too much like Psych 101, consider trying to work in a dysfunctional organization—an operation failing for a host of obvious reasons, but underlying every one is a manager who does not engage with his staff. In the absence of an engaged leader, employees vie for advantage, position, or attention, and continually fight and intrigue among themselves, even to the exclusion of doing their jobs. These problems disappear as trust is built with daily direction, consistent communication, and forcefully correcting inappropriate behavior.

If a manager doesn't understand this important point and fails to engage daily with all employees, he may be responsible for passively creating a hostile work environment. Such inattention to the daily functioning of the organization can be just as destructive as a supervisor who actively engages in demeaning, disparaging, and abusive behaviors.

ENGAGEMENT—

In a business sense engagement is the active involvement and commitment to one's enterprise, job, or task at hand.

If a leader wants his employees to engage with customers, he himself must engage with his employees. He can do this by his daily involvement in all that goes on in his department or section and by the continuing interaction and ongoing communication with those under his direction.

© 2009—Ed Rehkopf

Leadership on the Line
The Workbook

COMMUNICATION—

"The basic building block of good communications is the feeling that every human being is unique and of value."

Unknown

"The day soldiers stop bringing you their problems is the day you have stopped leading them."

General Colin Powell
U.S. Secretary of State,
Chairman of the Joint
Chiefs of Staff

"The art of communication is the language of leadership."

James Humes
Presidential Speech
Writer

© 2009—Ed Rehkopf

Exercise #5

Communication is of absolute importance to any organization, particularly in a people- and detail-intensive environment such as hospitality management or service enterprises. Not only must a leader communicate well with superiors, but also subordinates. She must always be open and accessible so employees feel no impediment to keeping her informed of problems and concerns. A front line leader, in particular, must stay engaged with her service team to know what is going on and to provide timely direction to her staff during the "heat" of daily operations.

Explain how a manager who gets angry or irritated when problems are brought to her attention negatively impacts the efficiency of the operation.

_____
_____
_____
_____

Put yourself in the place of an employee with a problem. What message is your manager sending you by becoming irritated when you come to her?

_____
_____
_____
_____

What tends to happen in an operation when employees hesitate telling their manager what's troubling them or what problems they're facing?

_____
_____
_____
_____

How can a Service-Based Leader overcome employees' natural hesitation to bring problems to their boss?

_____
_____
_____
_____

Lessons

Morale Matters!

In 1951 General Dwight David Eisenhower was tasked with the nearly overwhelming challenge of rallying the European democracies to the need for a common defense force—NATO—to counter the threat of the Soviet Union and its 175-division Red Army. The mood in the European capitals was one of deep pessimism. Having seen two world wars on their continent in a span of thirty years, having suffered death and destruction on a massive scale, facing home populations with deep distrust and antagonisms toward their neighbors—especially Germany—the situation was not promising for the necessary cooperation and effort to counter the Soviet menace.

While Eisenhower knew that the rearmament of Europe would be costly and take time, he saw as his greatest challenge the need to rebuild European morale and confidence. At the time he told diplomat Averell Harriman, "The last thing that a leader may be is pessimistic if he is to achieve success." In his diary he wrote, "Civilian leaders talk about the state of morale in a given country as if it were a sort of uncontrollable event or phenomenon, like a thunderstorm or a cold winter . . . (while) the soldier leader **looks on morale as the greatest of all his problems, but also as one about which he can and must do something."**

Morale has always been, and will always be, an important concern for military leaders. The effectiveness of their fighting force demands it. But it is not just in armies that morale is important. Athletic coaches know that dissension, bad attitudes, and pessimism will destroy all chances for victory, and they work hard to build the confidence and morale of their teams. The same is true in business or any group endeavor. Morale matters!

Attitude and morale are also important ingredients in hospitality and service operations where friendliness, good cheer, and enthusiasm are necessary requirements for success. While hiring the right people with the right personal qualities has always been a safe bet when building service teams, the very act of creating teams brings its own challenges. As pointed out in *Leadership and a Failure of Engagement*, the group dynamic often creates problems and can interfere with the smooth functioning of the work team.

So . . . just how does a leader go about ensuring good morale within his or her team? First and foremost, are the requirements of Service-Based Leadership—of the need to communicate well; of engaging daily with team members; listening to and addressing their concerns; providing the tools, resources, training, and support for employees to do their jobs well.

Beyond that is the need to recognize the ultimate value of people and act on that principle; to treat all employees with common decency; to lead by example and address concerns and problems promptly; and to be open and approachable for employees.

When all these things are done conscientiously and consistently by the leader, good morale is a natural by-product. **By focusing on being the best Service-Based Leader you can be, morale and its attendant *esprit* will come naturally.**

MORALE—

One dictionary defines morale as *"the moral or mental condition of a person or group with respect to cheerfulness, confidence, etc."*

Another says, *"the mental and emotional condition (as of enthusiasm, confidence, or loyalty) of an individual or group with regard to the function or tasks at hand; a sense of common purpose with respect to a group"* and *"the level of individual psychological well-being based on such factors as a sense of purpose and confidence in the future."*

A synonym is listed as *esprit de corps*—a French term dating from 1780 meaning, *"the common spirit existing in the members of a group and inspiring enthusiasm, devotion, and strong regard for the honor of the group."*

© 2009—Ed Rehkopf

Leadership on the Line
The Workbook

DOING THE RIGHT THING—

"Disciplining yourself to do what you know is right and important, although difficult, is the high road to pride, self esteem, and personal satisfaction."

Brian Tracy
Motivational Author and Speaker

Do the Right Thing

For any leader there will always be aspects of your job that you don't like—things that you personally find difficult or distasteful. And while there is always the temptation to postpone or ignore those things, hoping they will just go away or somehow solve themselves, this is seldom the case. Invariably, those neglected responsibilities come back full force at some later time—usually with far greater impact or consequence when they do.

Another mechanism to cope with these undesirable duties is to assign them to a subordinate or pass them off to some other person in the organization. While doing this may relieve your immediate distress, it is never a good thing to slough off your duties because they make you uncomfortable.

While undesirable duties will be different for each individual leader, these are some of the "usual suspects."

Confronting Poorly Performing Employees. Our basic nature is to assume that others know the right thing to do and will do it without being told. Clearly this mindset is not based in reality. People need to understand the right way of doing things and the standards of the organization. When they do not meet these expectations, you must engage them. Initially, these are ongoing discussions of what must be improved. Eventually, continued problems must lead to counseling and possibly disciplinary actions. A leader must never be hesitant to confront the problem employee. The sooner he does it, the better for everyone.

Discharging Employees. No normal person enjoys letting people go. Even when an employee deserves it for his inappropriate behavior or poor performance, it is never a pleasant thing to do. If, after exhausting all efforts to correct behavior or improve performance, the employee's problems persist, it is the right thing to do for the good of the organization and the other employees who have to put up with or cover for the offending employee.

Responding to Unhappy Customers. Does anybody enjoy this? However, it's probably one of the most important things you can do to ensure the success of your business. Recognizing that there will always be service failures, recovery is always the key. View these challenges as opportunities to demonstrate your leadership and professionalism. Well-handled, these situations can win you respect and admiration.

Reference-Checking when Hiring. Few of us enjoy the tedious time commitment and challenges of checking applicant references, yet there is nothing you can do that's more important for "getting the right people on your bus." This is a responsibility that you, as a leader and hiring manager, should never take lightly or pass off to someone else.

Speaking in Large Public Gatherings. Speaking in large gatherings causes many of us to cringe. Yet to grow leadership abilities and increase influence, don't shy away from these opportunities. The more you speak in public, the more comfortable you'll become doing it.

© 2009—Ed Rehkopf

(continued)

Lessons

While it's perfectly appropriate to delegate certain tasks as your career progresses and subsequent positions grow in authority, you must make sure delegation is appropriate and that your motivation is for the good of the organization, not based on what you like and dislike doing.

As a leader, you should never shy away from the responsibilities of the position you have accepted. Make it **a point of honor to do the right things**. Your employees are always watching and taking your measure as a leader. When you consistently do the right thing, you'll be seen as a "stand up" person—one who will always have their trust, respect, and loyalty.

Reflection: List some of the things you dislike or avoid doing. Think about each one and list steps you might take to lessen your aversion and make them easier to confront and accomplish.

RESPONSIBILITY—

"You cannot escape the responsibility of tomorrow by evading it today."

Abraham Lincoln
U.S. President

© 2009—Ed Rehkopf

Leadership on the Line
The Workbook

REGARD FOR PEOPLE—

"Your regard for people shines through in all of your actions and words. Your facial expression, your body language, and your words express what you are thinking about the people who report to you. Your goal is to demonstrate your appreciation for each person's unique value. No matter how an employee is performing on their current task, your value for the employee as a human being should never falter and always be visible."

Susan M. Heathfield
Business Consultant

Value Your People

What things can you as a leader do to demonstrate your regard for people "in all your actions and words"?

Know and use employee names. Everyone likes to be recognized as an individual and called by name. Certainly your regular customers do and your employees do as well. Introduce them to customers and visitors when appropriate. Failing to do so implies they're just part of the scenery instead of key contributors to the success of your operation.

Learn about employees as individuals. Get to know them, their life situations, their dreams and plans, their goals in life. This does not mean you are to become their friend or confidante, but it does mean you have enough interest in them as individuals to try to understand their situation, their needs, and motivations.

Greet employees daily. You should never fail to greet employees when you see them each day. You don't like to be ignored as if you were unimportant, and neither do they.

Share your time with employees. As busy as you are, make time for your employees. They have questions, concerns, and needs that should never be ignored. Be open and approachable. When you are not, when they are afraid to come to you for fear of your reaction, you are kept in the dark about what is really going on in your team. If any employee is monopolizing your time or is a "high maintenance" employee, do not be shy about letting him know the inappropriateness of this behavior.

Recognize each person's strengths and weaknesses. None of us is the perfect manager, server, retail attendant, etc. Don't expect your employees to be. Learn each person's strengths and weakness. Capitalize on the strengths and help each person overcome their weaknesses. The time you invest in helping an employee develop his or her skills and abilities is well worth the effort and will be appreciated far more than you'll ever realize.

Be involved in the workplace and work processes. Do not create a hostile work environment by failing to adequately engage with your employees. Without your ongoing guidance and direction, petty dissensions and friction will grow among the workers of your team as they struggle to figure out who must do what.

Look out for your peoples' welfare. Make sure your employees get adequate work breaks, that their workspaces are set up for comfort and efficiency, that they are properly trained and equipped for their jobs, that you adjust work schedules when possible to meet individual needs, that you resolve pay discrepancies quickly, that you get back to them to resolve issues they've raised. Make sure they understand their benefits, taking the time to explain the details to them.

Treat employees as adults. When you treat employees like children, they will act like children. Don't talk down to them or treat them as if they're immature. When you give people responsibility, most will reward your trust. Those who demonstrate they can't be trusted should be encouraged to move on.

Show respect. This is critically important in the way you speak, the tone of your voice, your choice of words, and your body language. Your respect for others cannot be faked. You must sincerely value people to treat them with respect at all times.

© 2009—Ed Rehkopf

(continued)

Lessons

Do not take advantage of people. Employees are not your servants and should not be expected to perform personal services for you. If you delegate tasks, make sure there is value in it for them, either in enhanced compensation or a genuine learning opportunity.

Demonstrate the common decencies of human interaction in all your dealings. Be kind and courteous. Give your people the benefit of the doubt. Don't be quick to take offense or become upset. Maintain control of your temper and reaction to events.

Thank employees often. How easy is it to say "Thank you"? It costs nothing and it reaps great rewards. The only requirement is that it must be sincerely given.

Say goodbye at the end of the day or shift. A farewell is a common courtesy that you would extend to family and friends, if for no other reason than as an acknowledgement of departure. The members of your work team, who you depend on for your success, should receive no less a courtesy. Again, the need for sincerity is absolute.

COMMON DECENCY—

Decency, noun. The state of being decent.

Decent, adjective. 1. Conforming to the recognized standard of propriety, good taste, modesty, etc., as in behavior or speech. 2. Kind; obliging; generous.

Dictionary.com

PEOPLE WILL—

"People will forget what you said, people will forget what you did, but people will never forget how you made them feel."

Maya Angelou
American Poet and Author

© 2009—Ed Rehkopf

LEADERSHIP—

"Leadership is action, not position."

Donald H. McGannon
President and Chairman
Westinghouse Broadcasting Company

Leadership on the Line
The Workbook

APPLICATIONS—

While leadership is the basis for effective relationships with your various constituencies, you must still demonstrate that leadership in the application of your management skills and techniques. The following applications will help you consider ways to lead and manage more effectively.

What You Owe Your Boss—Loyalty and Support	56
Managing Your Boss	57
Disciplined Hiring	58
Why the Wrong People Are Hired	59
Creating a Lasting Organizational Culture	61
Standards, Policies, and Procedures	63
Training	65
Personal Productivity	67
Planning and Review	69
Continual Process Improvement	70
Managers' Fiscal Responsibilities	71
Benchmarking	73
Performance Reviews	74
Exercise #6	76
Steps to Lower Employee Turnover	77
Employee Empowerment	78
The Distinction between Empowerment and Discretion	79
The Many Ways to "Kill" Empowerment	80

Leadership Applications

Notes

Leadership on the Line
The Workbook — Applications

What You Owe Your Boss—Loyalty and Support

In *Leadership on the Line*, we talked about managing your boss with a "State of the Union" report, timely and accurate information about your plans and projects, as well as the progress of your initiatives. In doing these things you keep your boss informed and assured that you are properly attending to the needs and requirements of your position. The ultimate purpose of managing your boss is to make her job easier, allowing her to focus on the other pressing issues of her position. Beyond this, what do you "owe" your boss? Most importantly you owe her your undivided loyalty and complete support.

Hopefully your boss is an active and engaged leader who has a plan of improvement and works diligently toward its implementation. In the process of implementing her agenda she will develop plans and programs and issue directives for their accomplishment. It is your responsibility and duty, then, to wholeheartedly support her agenda in its thorough implementation within your area of the operation.

But what if you have doubts about the wisdom or efficacy of her program? In this case you as a leader have a duty to fully and frankly express your reservations to her. However, this should always be done in private in a calm and deliberate way. Your purpose here is to convince, not attack or criticize. Clearly, rationally, and with suggestions for alternative courses of action, you must express your reservations and persuade your boss of other means to her desired ends.

If, after exhausting your powers of persuasion, your boss is unmoved and insists upon her original instructions, you have but two choices—to completely support and devote yourself 100% to accomplishing her directives or, if sufficiently opposed, to resign your position since you are unable to fully support her initiatives.

Why is the choice so stark? Is there no alternative between these two extremes? No! Either you fully support and implement her program without grumbling, complaining, or hesitation—as if the initiative were your own—or you step aside because you can't.

The most damaging thing you can do is to undermine your boss' efforts by publicly criticizing her plan or by failing to actively and aggressively implement it. Both send a clear message to your employees that you neither agree with nor support the plan. This will quickly set up divided loyalties in the workforce. Its impact on employees will be similar to the well-known phenomenon of parents sending mixed behavioral messages to their children.

Even worse is to pretend to support your boss' agenda while secretly acting to sabotage it. This passive-aggressive behavior is unfair to the person who hired you and is damaging to the organization. Your employees will readily understand your lack of commitment and ultimately your boss will recognize it too. In this instance, your boss' only recourse is to discharge you—and you will certainly deserve it.

The bottom line is that you have a responsibility to fully support and show loyalty to your boss. If, for whatever reason, you have come to lack respect for your boss, it's time for you to move on.

Still unconvinced? For one moment put yourself in the position of the boss—how long could you tolerate a subordinate manager who, either actively or passively, worked at cross purposes to your plans?

LOYALTY—

"If your boss demands loyalty, give him integrity. If your boss demands integrity, give him loyalty."

John Boyd

© 2009—Ed Rehkopf

Leadership on the Line
The Workbook

Managing Your Boss

As a leader, you are responsible for influencing your boss' perceptions of your work and performance. Keep your boss informed of the problems you're working on. Periodic summary reports showing operational trends, improved performance, and greater efficiencies keep her better informed and influence perceptions of your performance.

If you go to your boss with a problem, make sure you have a recommended solution. This allows her to agree with your thinking and problem-solving approach without being expected to do your job for you.

Also, the members of your service team will see how managing your boss enhances the team's stature in the eyes of higher management. Nothing is better for staff morale than knowing that your own supervisor is highly regarded by her superiors.

List and explain two things you might do to better manage your boss. Be specific!

1. _____

2. _____

ASSURE YOUR BOSS—

"Keep in mind that she has large responsibilities, is often very busy, and yet still has the need to know what is going on in the organization. Assuring your boss that you are aware of and actively working on problems sets her mind at ease."

Leadership on the Line

© 2009—Ed Rehkopf

Applications

Disciplined Hiring

Implied in Jim Collins' statement in the sidebar at left is the requirement that you **identify and only hire the right people.** The "wrong" people can be damaging to your business. Dr. Bradford Smart, in his book *Topgrading*, also speaks of hiring the right people, whom he calls high performers or "A-Players," as opposed to "B-" or "C-Players." Dr. Smart says,

> "High performers, the A-Players, contribute more, innovate more, work smarter, earn more trust, display more resourcefulness, take more initiative, develop better business strategies, articulate their vision more passionately, implement change more effectively, deliver higher quality work, demonstrate greater teamwork, and find ways to get the job done in less time with less cost."

Damage Caused by the Wrong Managers/Supervisors. Dr. Smart lists the many downsides of hiring and retaining C-Players as managers or supervisors. He says "C-Players:

- Embrace tradition over forward thinking.
- Have difficulty coping with new and complex situations.
- Prefer the status quo.
- Lack credibility, so others are hesitant to follow them.
- Require specific direction [from superiors].
- Hire mostly C-Players [A- and B-Players are seen as threats].
- Tolerate mediocrity.
- Have mediocre skills [and seldom seek self-improvement]."

Hiring and retaining low performing managers or supervisors can have long term negative effects which ripple through an organization. On the other hand, hiring A-Players for those critical leadership positions in a company can have significant and transformational positive effects.

Damage Caused by the Wrong Line Employees. If hiring the right people is particularly critical in hiring leaders, it is also important, though for different reasons, in hiring line employees—those who interface directly with customers. The dangers in hiring the wrong people in customer-interface positions include:

- The damage they can do to customer relations and service.
- The amount of time that you must spend in training and retraining them.
- The amount of time that you must spend in counseling, disciplining, and ultimately discharging them.
- The lost opportunity of using your limited time and resources to work with them—time that could be better spent on other initiatives and pressing issues.
- The cost of replacing a substandard employee—both in terms of hiring and training a replacement.
- And the emotional wear and tear on everyone involved.

HIRING THE RIGHT PEOPLE—

"The old adage 'People are your most important asset' is wrong. People are not your most important asset. The right people are."

Jim Collins
Good to Great, Why Some Companies Make the Leap…And Others Don't

© 2009—Ed Rehkopf

Leadership on the Line
The Workbook

HIRING THE WRONG PEOPLE—

"Managers who say, 'I don't have [time] for a [structured, chronological] interview,' should finish the sentence... 'so I will waste hundreds of hours when half the time I mis-hire people.'"

Bradford D. Smart
Topgrading, How Leading Companies Win by Hiring, Coaching, and Keeping the Best People

Why the Wrong People Are Hired

While there is no fail-safe method of hiring only the right people, there are common denominators underlying most mis-hires. They include:

Failure to Use Due Diligence. Given the responsibility managers have to hire the right people and avoid hiring the wrong people, hiring supervisors need to exercise "due diligence" throughout the hiring process. Due diligence is a financial/accounting term that means to conduct an investigation of a potential investment and/or confirm all material facts in regards to a sale.

Generally, due diligence refers to the care a reasonable person should take before entering into an agreement or a transaction with another party and is essentially a way of preventing unnecessary harm to either party involved in a transaction. While the term "due diligence" has come to take on the wider meaning of doing one's homework to prevent mistakes, clearly the original definition applies to hiring employees, that is making an offer of employment to another party.

Lack of Interview Skills. A brief informal survey of hospitality executives revealed that none has ever received formal training in how to screen and interview applicants or in reference-checking techniques. Despite the overwhelming importance of hiring the right people, it seems to be assumed that people can figure out for themselves how best to do it or will intrinsically know or possess such skills. Since Dr. Smart's research and experience points out that 50% of all hires are mis-hires, it is clear that this is not the case.

At the same time, a survey of hiring managers showed that most managers think they do a good job of interviewing job candidates. Given the sad hiring success rate, which is no better than flipping a coin, there is an obvious disconnect between hiring managers' perceptions and reality.

Not Taking Full Responsibility for the Hiring Process. There is only one person responsible for hiring the right people and that is the manager or supervisor of the person being hired. The hiring manager or supervisor is the one who is accountable for his department or section's performance and, therefore, is the only person who should make the hiring decision.

Never assume that hiring is the responsibility of a human resource department. They may assist in the process, but their assistance is consultative or clerical. If any person hired turns out to be a bust, the only person responsible and accountable is the hiring supervisor, and he must bear the consequences of mis-hiring.

Hiring a "Warm Body" to Fill a Position. There are times when there is a great sense of urgency to fill a key position. Often an empty managerial position puts a greater burden on other managers and the General Manager. There is also the well-known phenomena of the "spinning top." Without sufficient management to add the daily 'spin of leadership,' the operation soon begins to wobble and fall. As a result, hiring managers are keen to fill vacant leadership positions quickly. Despite these pressures, hiring managers should resist the temptation to hire a less-than-ideal candidate to quickly fill the vacant position.

Don't settle for less. At best you'll have a B-Player. At worst, you'll have someone that you'll need to spend hours and hours working with before letting him go, only to start over again.

© 2009—Ed Rehkopf

(continued)

Applications

Failure to Learn from Past Hiring Mistakes. While it is understood that every hiring manager will make some hiring mistakes, it is essential that lessons are learned from mis-hires. This can only be done if there is sufficient documentation of the hiring process. Without a written record that includes a resume or application, thorough interview notes including questions asked and answers given, and details of each reference checked, there is no way to go back after a mis-hire to try and determine what was missed during screening and interviewing.

With proper documentation, the hiring manager can review the entire screening, interviewing, and hiring process to see what signs were missed in an attempt to improve interview and reference-checking skills during future hires.

Summary. When you recognize why the wrong people are so often hired, you are in a position to do something about it.

- First and foremost, you should train yourself and your subordinate managers in proper screening, interviewing, and reference-checking techniques.
- Next, you should use various tools to help in the hiring process, such as interviewing and reference-checking forms.
- Lastly, you should establish and maintain a discipline of using the techniques and tools in all hiring situations.

Initially, Disciplined Hiring may take more time, but the more it is used, the easier the entire process will become.

MISTAKES—

"The only real mistake is the one from which we learn nothing."

John Powell

Leadership on the Line
The Workbook

ORGANIZATIONAL CULTURE—

The dictionary defines "culture" as *the sum total of ways of living built up by a group of human beings and transmitted from one generation to another.*

With a slight modification of this definition we come up with the following working definition of organizational culture:

The sum total ways of working and interacting built up by a group of people within an organization and transmitted from one generation of employees to another.

Creating a Lasting Organizational Culture

The major benefit of establishing an organizational culture is that once adopted by the majority of people in an organization, the culture takes on a life of its own and permeates the workplace. As normal turnover takes place, new hires quickly learn that to be accepted in their new surroundings, they must embrace the culture and make it their own.

In the absence of a culture developed, disseminated, and reinforced by the organization's leadership, a culture will arise on its own, usually fostered by a vocal few and often cynical and at odds with the purpose of the organization.

So how do you create a culture in your organization? First, you have to clearly and succinctly define the aims of your organization and what it aspires to be. These are most often found in Mission and Vision Statements.

Beyond these basic statements of intent, one must clearly spell out standards of behavior and performance. These can be in the form of Guiding Principles, Operating Standards, Leadership Principles, Service Ethic, Principles of Employee Relations, Organizational Values, Service Pocket Cards, a Code of Professional Ethics, or any other formal statements describing the "What, Why's, and How's" of conducting business.

Publishing such principles and statements, no matter how inspirational and well-written, will only foster employee cynicism if the values are not enthusiastically embraced by the organization's leadership. Conversely, when leaders demonstrate their commitment to the organization's values by their daily example, employees will do likewise.

With well-defined values and the enthusiastic example of leaders, the ground has been prepared for the fruits of organizational culture, but just as in growing a garden, preparing the soil is only the first step. The real work for a successful harvest is the daily tending—watering, fertilizing, pruning, weeding, and pest control.

In the case of an organizational culture, it is daily reinforcement at every opportunity with all employees that continues to focus individual attention on the values that underlie everyone's efforts. In some cases, it's publicly recognizing employees for embracing and utilizing the values in their work relationships or services rendered to customers. In other cases, it's privately correcting an employee who has ignored or transgressed the culture. In extreme cases, it's discharging the employee who refuses to accept the group norm. The key is to continually remind employees of the organization's values and elevate them from words on a page to an animating spirit that infuses every aspect of the organization and its work.

From the process of continually accentuating and reminding, the leader achieves a breakthrough. The breakthrough is reached when the organization reaches a critical mass of employee buy-in. Though the process of establishing an organizational culture requires patience and perseverance as well as leadership and example, when breakthrough is achieved, the culture takes over and is self-sustaining—with the employees holding the bar high and policing their own ranks.

In such an organization, employees understand what must be done and how. Motivation and morale are sky-high as employees are empowered by their participation and

(continued)

© 2009—Ed Rehkopf

Applications

contribution. The leader, relieved of the burden of constantly following behind employees to ensure they are doing the right things, can focus on strategic issues and the future of the organization.

The importance of a well-defined and promoted organizational culture cannot be overemphasized or underestimated in its impact on quality, performance, and customer service. The only thing that can screw it up is for the leader to fail to show an ongoing interest or fail to set an uncompromising example of the organizational culture and its values.

How would you describe the organizational culture at your company?

_____
_____
_____
_____

What steps, if any, has your company's leadership taken to define and implement an organizational culture? List any specific resources such as a mission and vision statement, employee handbook, service values, or standards of behavior.

_____
_____
_____
_____
_____
_____
_____
_____
_____
_____
_____
_____
_____
_____
_____
_____
_____

EIGHT STEPS TO A LASTING CULTURE—

1. Define and embrace values.
2. Set the example.
3. Constantly and enthusiastically remind and reinforce.
4. Indoctrinate new hires into culture.
5. Praise and reward those who uphold and foster the culture.
6. Correct, counsel, and, if necessary, discharge those who don't.
7. Do not let anyone, especially managers and supervisors, disparage or ignore the culture.
8. Preach the message at every opportunity.

© 2009—Ed Rehkopf

Leadership on the Line
The Workbook

DEFINITIONS—

Standard
- *Something considered by an authority or by general consent as a basis for comparison; an approved model.*
- *Anything as a rule or principle that is used as a basis or model for judgment.*
- *Morals, ethics, habits, etc., established by authority, custom, or an individual as acceptable.*
- *Fulfilling specific requirements as established by an authority, law, rule, custom, etc.*

Policy (ies)
- *A definite course of action adopted for the sake of expediency, facility, etc.*
- *Action or procedure conforming to or considered with reference to prudence or expediency.*
- *Prudence, practical wisdom, or expediency. (expedient: tending to promote some proposed or desired object; fit or suitable under the circumstances. Synonyms include advisable, appropriate, desirable.).*

Procedure (s)
- *An act or a manner of proceeding in any action or process; conduct.*
- *A particular course of mode of action.*

The Random House College Dictionary

Standards, Policies, and Procedures

The terms Standards, Policies, and Procedures are used in business to describe the what and how to's of a company's organization and work processes.

Standards. In a manufacturing setting product standards usually include material specifications, manufacturing tolerances, quality measurements, and the functionality of the finished product.

In the hospitality field or service industry, however, the establishment of a standard is usually made by management based upon an understanding or expectation of what will satisfy or impress the customer. Often this satisfaction is based upon the manner in which some service or action is performed. Therefore, the standard is a description of the desired outcome of that service or action and/or the manner in which it is performed, such as the approved way of presenting and opening a bottle of wine, or the correct way to fill out a form used for documenting personnel actions, the manner in which month-end inventories will be conducted, or the level of professionalism of management and operations.

Standards are established by the owners or general manager as the acceptable model of performance by which customers judge proficiency and professionalism. They apply not only to the daily performance of individual duties, but also to the manner in which employees conduct themselves.

Policies. Policies and standards are so closely interwoven it is often hard to tell them apart. Policies most often apply to those areas of the operation where they can be little or no leeway in how something is done, for instance in the area of human resources where so much is dictated by law and the need for correct action to avoid litigation, or in the area of accounting where exactness and consistency are necessary to ensure the correctness, accuracy, timeliness, and transparency of financial reporting and fiduciary responsibilities.

Policies can also apply to operations. Policies are established to ensure the consistent and fair treatment of customers; for instance there might be a policy for giving refunds or making dining reservations. The need for policy here is to ensure that every customer receives equal treatment and the same opportunity to use and enjoy the business and its products or services. Nothing will upset a customer faster than believing he or she is not getting a fair shake from the business. While human resources and accounting policies must be stringently followed, operating policies tend to be more flexible to meet changing customer needs.

Procedure (s). Procedures are the "how to's" of business. Sometimes they flow from standards and sometimes from policies, but in the end they are exact instructions of how to do or complete a particular process, act, or event. Whereas policies are often the reason why something is done, procedures are the detail of how it is done.

Example of Standards, Policies, and Procedures

Note the policies and procedures for taking a dining reservation below. Taken together they represent the standard of how to take a reservation and provide a description of the desired outcome of the process.

<u>Policies:</u>
1. *Reservations will be taken for all dining venues—casual dining, fine dining, and Sunday brunch.*

(continued)

© 2009—Ed Rehkopf

Applications

WHY WRITTEN STANDARDS, POLICIES, & PROCEDURES?—

It is essential to develop detailed, written standards, policies, and procedures for every area of operations. Not only are these the basis for developing training material, but they serve as the foundation for developing a culture of service that is consistently taught to new hires and reinforced by both management and other employees.

When everyone understands "the way things are done," there is less opportunity for freelance behavior. Eliminating freelancing or employee discretion fosters consistency of product and service delivery. As Harvard Professor Theodore Levitt says in his book, *Marketing for Business Growth*, "Discretion is the enemy of order, standardization, and quality."

In fact, employees will be the first to say that they appreciate the time and effort taken to teach them the accepted way of doing things and that management insists upon uniformly high standards. People naturally take pride in being associated with quality and this is true for any industry or endeavor.

2. *Reservations will be taken no earlier than 60 days in advance of a requested date.*
3. *A la carte reservations will not normally be taken for parties of more than 12. When an exception is made for a party of more than 12, the Dining Services Manager and Chef will coordinate a set or limited menu for the party.*
4. *The Dining Room Manager is responsible for maintaining the reservation book for all venues.*
5. *Reservations may be made by calling 555-5555, from 8 a.m. to 9 p.m. Tuesday through Friday, and 11 a.m. to 9 p.m. Saturday and Sunday.*
   a. *During normal office hours (8 a.m. to 5 p.m., Tuesday through Friday), reservation calls will be taken by the Receptionist.*
   b. *During all other hours, reservations will be forwarded to the dining room where they will be taken by the dining room Host or Hostess.*
   c. *Outside of normal reservation times, a voice mail message will inform customers of the hours that reservations may be taken and that a voice mail message will be returned promptly during normal business hours.*

<u>Procedures</u>
1. *Answer the phone in three rings.*
2. *Use a pleasant tone of voice to communicate your desire to help.*
3. *Answer the phone with "Good Morning/ Afternoon/ Evening, thank you for calling the main dining room, this is (your name). How may I help you?"*
   Note: It is important to get the name of the caller first, so that you may address him/her by name during the rest of the call.
4. *If you must place the caller on hold, say "Mr./Mrs. (customer name), may I place you on hold for a moment?"*
   a. *If the answer is yes, say "Thank You" and place the caller on hold.*
   b. *If the answer is no, continue with the call.*
5. *Obtain all necessary information: day/date of reservation, time, number in party, and customer phone number.*
6. *Ask for special needs, accommodations, or if they are celebrating a special occasion.*
7. *Read back the information you have taken to ensure all information is accurate.*
8. *Thank the customer for calling.*

Standards, Policies, and Procedures form the bulk of the material that an employee must master to satisfactorily complete all their job functions, duties, and responsibilities. Without taking the time to define, explain, and clarify standards, policies, and procedures, how can management realistically know what it is that employees need to learn? Without well-defined (i.e., written and reviewed) standards, policies, and procedures, any attempt to train will be disorganized and inconsistent.

While department heads and junior managers are typically responsible for developing the operating standards, policies, and procedures for their departments, the general manager is still responsible for ensuring the overall quality of the operation and must therefore review all operating standards, policies, and procedures. He can only do this if they are in writing and available for his review.

© 2009—Ed Rehkopf

Leadership on the Line
The Workbook

TRAINING—

"It is the responsibility of leaders at all levels of the business to ensure that employees are developed to their fullest potential and that they are trained in all aspects of their jobs. Because most businesses are large and complex, involving hundreds of details, there is much for employees to know.

From the company's perspective, the desired outcome of the hiring process is to hire, train, and retain quality people who will make a positive contribution to the success of the enterprise. As leaders, you have a vested interest in the success of your employees. You want them to succeed because they will help you succeed.

The surest way to guarantee their success is to create the environment and programs that ensure the fullest development of their potential. This development of the abilities and skills of employees is an ongoing process requiring your continual interest and active participation."

Leadership on the Line

© 2009—Ed Rehkopf

Training

All of us who work in the service business understand that operations are both people-intensive and detail-intensive. It takes a lot of employees to provide the requisite levels of service and every aspect of service involves many details. These two facts make detailed, ongoing training an absolute necessity for any successful operation.

Types of Training. There are a wide variety of topics that must be taught to both managers and employees to fully prepare them for their jobs.

1. **Leadership Development** Training for managers and supervisors—designed to teach consistent, company-wide leadership skills, which are the driving force behind the company's success.
2. **Organizational Systems** Training such as Human Resource and Accounting Standards, Policies, and Procedures for managers and supervisors—designed to teach the underlying systems that permit the enterprise to operate efficiently.
3. **Company Culture** Training for all employees—designed to foster a thorough understanding of the company's values and service ethic.
4. **Legal Compliance** Training for managers, supervisors, and employees—designed to provide all required training in matters with legal implications for the company such as Equal Employment Opportunity, Fair Labor Standards Act, Sexual Harassment, and others.
5. **Liability Abatement** Training for managers, supervisors, and employees—designed to limit the company's liability exposure for Occupational Safety and Health, food sanitation, or product safety.
6. **Service Technique** Training for employees—designed to give each employee the skill set necessary to perform his job and meet high standards of service.

Items 1 through 5 above should be developed by the company and provided company-wide for consistency sake; item 6 is specific to each department and should be developed and taught by individual department heads.

Prerequisite to Training. Before establishing training requirements and materials, you must determine in great depth a company's operating standards, policies, and procedures. These are, after all, the backbone of any organized system of training.

Requirements for a Successful Training Program. Certain things are necessary in order for your training program to be successful:

- Leadership—the will to make it happen.
- The necessary focus and attention.
- Designated responsibilities and accountabilities.
- Established training objectives, standards, guidance, and budget.
- Administrative system or software to monitor and track training compliance.
- Training benchmarks and reports to track time and costs of training effort.
- Standardized list of teaching aids and equipment to facilitate training.

Training Principles. There are a number of principles which guide the development and implementation of a business' training plan:

(continued)

Applications

A DAILY HUDDLE—

The Ritz-Carlton Hotel Company, renowned for its "legendary service," reinforces its service principles every day during every shift in every one of their properties world-wide. Every employee, from senior executive to most recently hired worker, attends the "Daily Line-up" where values are discussed.

Compare this Daily Line-up with the habits of professional athletes, whose jobs require peak performance, both individually and as a team, in an environment where "winning isn't everything, it's the only thing!" Without fail, these athletes huddle for a few moments before every game to remind themselves of their commitment to each other and their mission to win.

In the service business our game is every day, every shift, but isn't our need to "win" just as important?

© 2009—Ed Rehkopf

- Not all employees learn equally well or fast; and not all employees find the same teaching techniques conducive to learning. Therefore, you need to develop training formats that meet the needs of all learners. Such formats will include self-study manuals, checklists, handouts, quizzes, DVDs, Power Point presentations, "on-the-go" training material, scripting of key customer interfaces, and ongoing discussions at staff meetings.
- Training employees is not a one-time task. New employees must receive initial training, but the amount of material that must be mastered requires that ongoing and refresher training be given in most topics and job skills.
- Some sort of Daily Huddle should be used by every department every shift to inspect staff, remind them of important service details, provide "on-the-go" training, and ensure every employee has the proper mind-set and enthusiasm to deliver high levels of service.
- Some training such as discrimination, sexual harassment, and safety training is required by law. Because of legal and liability issues, such training must be consistently taught throughout the company and such training thoroughly documented.
- All individuals tasked with training responsibilities must be trained. Completing a Train the Trainer class is a prerequisite to training other employees.

Strategies for Meeting Training Requirements. The following are suggested to help managers allocate the necessary time and resources for training:

- Incremental training—review the curriculum for each position. If there are 30 topics to be covered each year, break the training down into one lesson per week or two lessons every two weeks or five per month. By spreading the training burden over time, the amount that needs to be taught in any given week is lessened.
- Schedule in advance—plan and schedule a full year's training in advance so busy and slow periods can be noted and taken into account when scheduling training. Every so many weeks schedule an open training day that can be used to catch up when unforeseen levels of business force postponement of classes.
- Take advantage of traditionally slow times (identified by benchmarking revenues) to schedule the bulk of the training or instruction that takes longer to provide.
- Establish standard training days and times—this helps make training routine for both the instructor and employees.
- Use the Daily Huddle to take advantage of "on-the-go" training material to give short training sessions. On-the-go material can also be used whenever unexpected windows of time open up.
- Consider charging training hours to a General & Administrative account instead of to each department. Charging them to departments may prove a disincentive to train when managers' bonus calculations include controlling payroll costs.
- Benchmark all training sessions—track topics, dates, times, how many in attendance, as this will help establish a more efficient schedule for future years.

The Challenge. In establishing a formal discipline of training you are undertaking an extremely challenging endeavor—one that will demand your focused and persistent attention. While it adds a number of time-consuming tasks to an already busy schedule, it ultimately will make your job easier as the quality and efficiency of your operation improve. You can expect that problems and obstacles will arise as you press ahead with this challenging initiative, but with your continued "will to make it happen" success will surely follow.

Leadership on the Line
The Workbook

Personal Productivity

Leading in a service environment is demanding and time-consuming. Managers and supervisors at all levels too often find themselves reacting to events and constantly responding to the crisis of the moment.

What all this means is that in order to stay ahead of this never-ending press of daily operations and to attend to the many important issues of customer service, organization and operating efficiencies, special events and activity programming, planning and review, staff development and training, and continual process improvement, not to mention life/work balance and personal sanity, a manager must be well-organized and highly productive. Below are some of the strategies and habits that can improve your personal productivity.

Annual Planning. Have an annual plan and timelines for your department or section. Put it in writing to commit to its accomplishment and review it on a monthly basis.

Work Planning. Your personal work plan will include what steps need to be taken to meet your departmental goals, but will also have personal goals, such as developing yourself and your skill set.

Use a Day-Timer to better organize yourself, your schedule, and your daily tasks. Use it to look and plan ahead.

Make Lists and Prioritize. Priorities change frequently—even on a daily basis—but keep a list of priorities (1. *Critical—must be accomplished as soon as possible; 2. Priority—must be accomplished; 3. Routine—will be accomplished as time and resources permit*).

Develop and Use Checklists. These pre-prepared lists for project work, such as organizing storage areas or deep cleaning work spaces, can be used to assign your employees recurring tasks when business is slow, but you are not yet prepared to send anyone home.

Plan Ahead. The planning horizons may vary from department to department, but you should always be looking ahead at least three month (and often 5 to 6 months) for special events, seasonal activities, increasing or decreasing business levels, vacation scheduling, and any other events or activities that require advance planning.

Use a Personal Computer. The PC is a great productivity tool and standard business word processing, spreadsheet, and graphics software, such as MS-Office®, will allow you to create professional-looking documents that can be stored for future use or modification, such as written standards, policies, and procedures; training materials; budgets and benchmarks; and room diagrams. Having these skills will not only make you more productive and help you communicate more professionally, but will significantly enhance your career opportunities and advancement.

Organize and Save Your Work. As you produce written standards, policies, and procedures; training materials; various communications; specialized spreadsheets; and any other intellectual material on the computer, save them for future use. Most of what you spend time to create you'll use again as you progress through your career, but you must be able to find it.

(continued)

PERSONAL NOTE—

Attending the Military Academy at West Point was a great personal organizer. Starting with Beast Barracks and continuing through four years, cadets are given far more to do every day than could humanly be accomplished. In order to survive, we quickly learned how to be efficient, how to use even spare moments of downtime to prepare for requirements later in the day or tomorrow.

We also learned pretty quickly to prioritize—again, as a matter of survival. While everything was said to be important, it didn't take too long to recognize that some things were more important than others. Four years of these constant pressures make Academy graduates pretty good at organizing themselves and their time.

While not many get the benefit of this experience, the pressures of the hospitality business or service sector are not unlike those at the Academy. In our industry there is far more to accomplish every day than time or stamina permit. But rather than be overwhelmed by this daily burden, the smart leader will use it as motivation to get better organized.

© 2009—Ed Rehkopf

Applications

Benchmark Your Operation and Forecast Business Levels. Benchmarking will give you a deeper understanding of your business and its seasonality and will help you budget more accurately for future years. It will also allow you to formally forecast upcoming business levels, allowing more efficient staffing. Both of these disciplines will help take some of the guesswork out of your business decisions.

Master and Delegate Routine Tasks. Routine tasks such as setting schedules, ordering consumable supplies, benchmarking, formal forecasting, and others can and should be delegated to competent and conscientious employees. You must still supervise the work and check its accuracy on a regular basis, but you'll save your own time while helping develop the confidence and abilities of one or more of your employees. Be sure the selected employees are also benefiting by the arrangement through genuine learning opportunity or possibly additional compensation for the tasks.

But before you delegate any task to another, make sure you have mastered the task yourself, have a complete understanding of any and all issues involved, and train the selected employee thoroughly—not just by showing her how, but by explaining why at the same time.

Establish Daily, Weekly, Monthly, Seasonal, and Annual Habits. The above disciplines will be far easier to implement if you establish regular schedules to do some of the following:

- Daily—Benchmarking, staff communication, continual ongoing reviews of your operation, monitoring payroll hours.
- Weekly—Payroll verification, forecasting, staff scheduling, reviewing and planning for upcoming events, Tools to Beat Budget (i.e., some sort of process to track expenses versus budget in real time), coding invoices, ordering supplies and inventories, ongoing staff training.
- Monthly—Inventories, Tools to Beat Budget, monthly review of operating statements and work plans, continual process improvement.
- Seasonal—Event and activity programming, seasonal hiring and terminations, ordering seasonal supplies and inventories.
- Annual—Planning, budgeting, asset inventory.

Summary. Your department's or section's organization and efficiency starts and ends with you. The efficiency of your operational area and your employees' work habits will reflect your personal productivity. To the extent you are disorganized, undisciplined, and work without a plan, your area of the operation will follow suit.

SOLUTIONS—

"Never complain—always occupy yourself with solutions."

Leadership on the Line

© 2009—Ed Rehkopf

Leadership on the Line
The Workbook

Planning and Review

Every enterprise demands a plan. Without a **formal, written plan** to focus attention and action on the completion of specified goals within a specified time period, the enterprise will lack clear direction and purpose. Planning for operations should include:

- A Strategic Plan covering a period of 3 to 5 years, updated annually. This plan looks at the company's strengths, weaknesses, threats, and opportunities. Its primary purpose is to ensure its competitive position in the marketplace. Strategic Planning is also a tool to focus owners on a long-term approach to guiding the business, as well as a means to plan for capital improvements or replacement in an orderly manner.

- An Annual Plan covering a period of 12 months, coinciding with the budgeting cycle. This plan lays out the specific goals to be accomplished during the year as part of efforts toward continual improvement and meeting the requirements of the Strategic Plan.

- A General Manager's Work Plan for the 12 months covered by the Annual Plan. This plan lays out measurable accountabilities for the general manager and is the basis for her performance appraisal.

- A Work Plan for each department head for the same 12 months. These plans do the same for department heads.

- Plans for major projects and events. These are plans developed for specific major tasks or activities such as purchasing new equipment, renovating a facility, or preparing for major annual events.

Without work plans it is impossible to **hold managers accountable** for their work and the performance of their departments or the business as a whole.

Given the extensive nature of planning requirements, the company must carefully define its planning process, responsibilities, and timeline, and all managers must be required to develop "stretch" plans for their areas of responsibility.

The ongoing review of operations and the necessity to monitor progress toward work plan accomplishment is just as important as the requirement to plan. A monthly discipline of having department heads meet with the general manager to review their operating performance and work plan completion will help the general manager keep in close contact with each department's progress.

PLANNING—

"The importance of disciplined planning cannot be overstated. Haphazard planning results in haphazard operations and equally haphazard performance."

Ed Rehkopf
The Quest for Remarkable Service

REVIEW—

"Coming full circle, there must be ongoing formal review of the operations. Were plans completed? What worked and what didn't? What are the benchmarks telling us? Careful review and analysis of all areas of the operation at every level by every manager will help the company achieve Continual Process Improvement."

Ed Rehkopf
The Quest for Remarkable Service

© 2009—Ed Rehkopf

Applications

Continual Process Improvement

The sailor at sea must make constant adjustment to his sails, the tension of his rigging, and the set of his rudder to maintain optimum performance and to avoid disaster. He must do this because everything around him is changing—the weather, direction and force of the wind, current, direction and height of the waves, direction and distance to shoals and reefs, and the course he needs to sail. Without his ongoing attention, he will certainly run into trouble.

This analogy is a good one for life in general and business in particular. Everything changes—all the time. This is true of your marketplace, your competitors, your customers, and your employees. To ensure that you and your company are prepared for change, you must constantly review your operation and continually make adjustments to optimize performance.

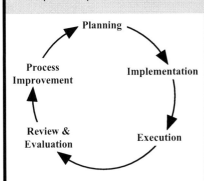

CONTINUAL PROCESS IMPROVEMENT
"The Discipline of Quality"

Failing to do so is a sign of laziness at worst and poor time management at best. Without a discipline of continual process improvement you condemn your organization to a course of never-ending reaction to the forces around you. In this case, your agenda and that of your team is no longer yours, it is determined by ever-changing events. The bottom line is that you are no longer leading your team, you are simply reacting to the storm around you.

But it doesn't have to be this way. Assert your control over the situation by continually reviewing the various aspects of your operation to ensure that things are being done in the optimum way and that everything is functioning smoothly. How can you do this?

Be engaged in your operation. Your daily involvement in your department or section is the best way to know what's going on and what needs your attention.

Monitor your operation. In particular pay attention to problems and issues. These are the clear indicators of what needs to be reviewed in detail.

Encourage your employees to bring their issues and problems to you. These will often point directly to things that need to be improved. Make sure you create the environment where employees know they are appreciated for doing this. If you get irritated or angry every time they bring a concern, they will soon stop coming to you.

Establish a culture of review and improvement. Central to this is a mindset of problem discovery and solution. When your employees see you solving the problems they deal with every day, they will jump on the bandwagon to help.

Set aside time to review. Schedule weekly and monthly reviews of problem areas. Then come up with solutions to resolve problems. Establish an annual plan to review one "hot spot" of your operation each month to continually stay ahead of issues.

Formally review ongoing activities and events. Do a *post mortem* on any ongoing activities. Involve your employees to determine what worked and what didn't. Solicit their ideas for improvement. Keep a written record of your review for future use.

As time-consuming as you think continual process improvement may be, think of the consequences of failing to do it—in the long run you'll spend far more time reacting to disasters. And sadly, they'll be disasters of your own making!

CONTINUAL PROCESS IMPROVEMENT—

"Given the many details associated with managing a quality operation, it is imperative that management commit to and promote a process of continual improvement in all areas of the operation.

This requires a positive emphasis on problem discovery, a discipline of constant review, and an understanding that in quality service operations, the devil is in the details. As more and more areas of the operation become systematized and routine, management at all levels, with the commitment and assistance of their empowered employees, must continually 'peel the onion' to deeper and deeper layers of detail.

Further, no detail must be seen as too trivial to warrant management's attention and the establishment of standards and procedures to ensure it is consistently attended to by the staff."

Ed Rehkopf
The Quest for Remarkable Service

© 2009—Ed Rehkopf

Leadership on the Line
The Workbook

Managers' Fiscal Responsibilities

Managers with bottom-line responsibility are responsible for the financial performance of their areas of the operation. There are a number of specific elements associated with this responsibility, which are broken down into the following broad categories:

Budgeting. Budgeting is the process of establishing a financial operating and capital plan for a future fiscal year. Budgets are formulated using past history, benchmarks, knowledge of upcoming events or trends, and one's best professional judgment.

Comparing Actual Performance to Budget. Once approved, budgets are the fiscal plan for the year. Managers are responsible for comparing actual performance to budgets on a monthly basis and intervening as necessary to achieve budget goals.

Achieving Revenues. Achieving revenue projections is one of the two primary means of meeting budgets (the other being controlling expenses). Managers are responsible for monitoring revenues and aggressively intervening when revenues fall short.

Controlling Cost of Goods Sold. Departments with retail operations must also control the cost of goods sold and investigate when these costs are out-of-line. Managers can do this by ensuring accurate monthly inventories, carefully tracking departmental transfers and adjustments, and using retail buying plans.

Controlling Payroll Costs. Payroll is the single largest expense in most operations and the most significant expense that managers must control. In order to control payroll costs, it is vital that managers have timely and accurate data regarding their departmental payroll costs. Essential to getting this data is having staff correctly follow timekeeping procedures, setting schedules to meet forecasted levels of business, and the dogged determination to track payroll expenses closely to ensure that budgets are not exceeded.

Controlling Other Expenses. Other Expenses comprise all of the other departmental operating expenses. Managers can control these expenses by carefully reviewing expenditures on a monthly basis, using some means, such as Tools to Beat Budget, to track other expenses in real time, and by periodic in-depth reviews of significant expense accounts.

Benchmarking. Benchmarking is the act of measuring operating performance. Each department head should track detailed benchmarks for his area of the operation

Pricing. The starting point for meeting revenue projections is proper pricing of products and services to ensure a sufficient markup to cover associated expenses. Pricing should be reviewed on a periodic basis to assure that budgeted margins are being maintained.

Purchasing. Some managers are responsible for purchasing materials, supplies, and inventories for their departments. Managers must be familiar with all company purchasing policies to properly fulfill these responsibilities.

Expense Coding. Managers are sometimes responsible for ensuring that invoices for all purchased items are coded to appropriate expense accounts in a timely, accurate, and consistent manner.

RESPONSIBILITY TO SHAREHOLDERS—

"Whether a company is privately or publicly owned, the shareholders are the owners of the enterprise. They have invested their money in the venture with the expectation of receiving a return on their investment. Without shareholders and their willingness to assume risks, you and your team would not have a job.

Often a company's shareholders are removed from the operation. They allow professional managers to run the day-to-day business of the company. But even if they are seldom or never on the premises, this does not mean that they do not have needs to be met.

While you may have little opportunity to directly serve shareholders, everything you do to serve the company's customers and everything you do to better organize and operate the enterprise does have a direct bearing on satisfying your shareholders."

Leadership on the Line

© 2009—Ed Rehkopf

(continued)

Applications

PROTECTING SHAREHOLDERS' ASSETS—

"Safeguarding the company's assets begins with the leadership and integrity of its supervisors. First and foremost, you should set an unimpeachable example for your employees. If they see that you are careless with company property, that you take advantage of your position, that you appropriate company assets for personal use, that you are more concerned about your perquisites than the welfare of the company, they will find countless ways to do the same."

Leadership on the Line

Inventory Management and Security. Given that high inventory levels tie up capital that might be put to better use elsewhere, managers must use common sense and good business judgment to maintain inventories at levels that balance business demands, lower pricing for bulk purchases, perishability of stock, and available warehousing space.

Inventories must be kept secured with access limited to as few individuals as possible. Storerooms must be kept neat, clean, and organized to facilitate physical inventory counts and minimize damage and spoilage.

Merchandise inventories should be purchased using Open to Buy or other retail buying plans, thereby constantly monitoring inventory levels and product mix while minimizing markdowns. All special sales of merchandise during the year should be noted and marked-down items analyzed compared to buying plans to ensure that lessons are learned from buying mistakes.

Asset Management. Managers are responsible for protecting the assets assigned to their departments and in their care.

Periodic physical counts are required for assets under your control:
- Resale inventories—monthly to determine cost of goods sold.
- Supply inventories, such as linens, china, glassware—quarterly to ensure you have sufficient stock on hand. Some consumable items, such as warewashing chemicals, cleaning supplies, and paper products should be inventoried more frequently.
- Furniture, Fixtures, and Equipment inventories—to ensure presence and accountability.

Internal Controls. Internal Controls are defined as the systems and procedures established and maintained to safeguard a business' assets, check the accuracy and reliability of its accounting data, promote operational efficiency, and encourage adherence to prescribed managerial policies.

Internal controls, while often considered an accounting function, are actually a function of management. The ultimate responsibility for good internal controls rests squarely with managers.

Point of Sale (POS) Transactions. The initial entry for most revenue data is through point of sale systems. Managers are responsible for training their employees to correctly use the POS system and to retrain as necessary when a pattern of errors is evident in their departments.

Accounting Standards, Policies, and Procedures. Managers should be familiar with and follow all requirements of their company's accounting standards, policies, and procedures and recommend changes as necessary.

Summary. The thoroughness and professionalism with which you meet these fiscal responsibilities will have much to do with your success as a manager. Consider which ones you currently do well and in which areas you need to improve your performance.

© 2009—Ed Rehkopf

Leadership on the Line
The Workbook

BENCHMARKING—

"Imagine two professional baseball teams. One team measures every aspect of every player's performance—the number of at bats; number of hits, walks, and strikeouts; batting averages against right- and left-handed pitchers; slugging averages; and fielding percentages. They also measure each pitcher's earned run average, number of base on balls, strikeouts, wild pitches; and so on. The other team decides it's too much trouble and keeps no statistics whatsoever.

These two teams will meet each other eighteen times a season. While well matched in player talent, hustle, and desire, and though each team possesses competent management and coaching, one team dominates the other season after season. Would anyone be surprised to discover which is the dominant team?

As everyone knows, this example is ludicrous because every baseball team measures players' performance and uses this information to make crucial game decisions. What is it that baseball managers understand that some business owners and managers don't seem to grasp? The fact that everything in life follows patterns. When patterns are tracked and analyzed, they can be used to predict future performance and set goals."

Leadership on the Line

© 2009—Ed Rehkopf

Benchmarking

Benchmarking, the act of measuring and analyzing operating performance, seeks to understand the patterns underlying a company's operation. Reasons to benchmark include:

- Benchmarks can be used to **establish performance goals** for future operating periods.
- Benchmarks help **identify under-performance and best practices**.
- Benchmarks from past periods can **make budgeting for future periods easier and far more accurate**.
- Tracking revenues and comparing them to historical benchmarks allows management to **measure customer response** to products/services and new initiatives.
- Benchmarks create the **measurable accountabilities** for each manager's work plan.

The company's monthly operating statements provide good basic information, but these summary numbers can mask troubling trends within the operation. For instance, higher food revenues in a restaurant can be a result of less patronage, but each customer spending more because of higher menu prices. The manager is happy with the higher revenues, but is blissfully ignorant of declining clientele.

Benchmarking is best accomplished by department heads who have bottom line responsibility. Most performance measures will fall into the following broad categories.

- Revenues and expenses, both aggregate and by individual category
- Inventories
- Retail sales mix to determine buying patterns of customers

Most of the raw data necessary to benchmark comes from point-of-sale reports. Much of this lode of daily information gets looked at briefly by department heads or the accounting office and is then filed away, rarely to be seen again. The real value of this information comes from tracking it over time to determine trends by day of week, week to week, month to month, and year to year. This makes it necessary for managers to pull the information from POS reports and enter it into spreadsheet software.

A few caveats:

- There are as many aspects of an operation to measure as time, resources, and ingenuity will allow. Focus on those most critical to one's operation.
- Data used in benchmarking must be defined and collected in a consistent manner.
- When comparing data, always compare like to like.
- Ensure benchmarks measure events with only one underlying variable.
- Do not draw conclusions from too small a sample. The larger the sample, the more accurate the conclusions.
- When two pieces of data are compared to generate a benchmark, both a small sample size or extreme volatility in one or the other, can skew the resultant benchmark.

Benchmarking is not complicated, but it does require discipline and persistence. It is best accomplished by setting up routine systems to collect, compile, report, and analyze the information collected. Like a baseball team, the knowledge gained by benchmarking will bring a company to the top of its game.

Applications

Performance Reviews

Performance reviews are periodic, formal feedback sessions that help measure an employee's contribution to the overall effort.

Reviews give important feedback to employees, reinforcing those things they do well while helping them improve in areas where their performance is weak. As such, they are part of the ongoing training effort of the company.

Performance reviews must include an opportunity for the employee to give feedback as well. A performance review should be a dialogue with nothing finalized until the session is ended.

The Performance Review Concept

Prior to a performance review, a supervisor must explain to an employee the criteria by which his performance will be judged. This is only fair, as everyone deserves to know those things by which their work will be evaluated. The perfect time to share and explain the Performance Review form is upon hiring when the supervisor provides the employee a job description and explains the functions of the position.

The purpose of any performance review is to obtain the best possible performance from each employee by positively reinforcing desired skills and behaviors, while developing his full potential by coaching and constructively correcting those behaviors that need improvement. The basic concepts behind achieving optimum performance from each employee are to:

- Set goals and expectations the first day of employment and adjust and reinforce them during the entire period of employment.
- Coach along the way, correcting when necessary and reinforcing positive performance.
- Ensure that any performance review is not a monologue by the supervisor; rather it should be a dialogue between the employee and supervisor to reach a mutual understanding of what optimum performance is and how to achieve it.
- Set goals for the next session and discuss how to accomplish them.

Conducting a Meaningful Performance Review

Performance reviews are only as meaningful and useful as the effort put into them by the supervisor. The following guidelines are provided to help supervisors understand the basic requirements for conducting meaningful performance reviews.

Preparation

- Prepare for the performance discussion. Schedule a quiet place, make sure you have enough time, and don't allow interruptions.
- Using information gathered from Staff Notes (see sidebar on the next page), your recollection of events, records of employee counseling, as well as comments from other leaders and customers, organize your thoughts and make an outline of the topics you wish to discuss. Be thorough. Your preparation is key to a successful dialogue and outcome.

(continued)

PERFORMANCE REVIEWS—

Reviews must be based on specific facts, not generalities. Managers should keep notes throughout the review period on the strengths and deficiencies of an employee's work. If this is done, a manager will be able to provide a meaningful review based on actual fact and will be able to give relevant examples to the employee to ensure he understands.

Reviews should be honest, fair, and candid. No manager should attempt to avoid conflict with an employee by giving an overly positive evaluation. Such an evaluation could be used as evidence of satisfaction with his work in a wrongful termination case.

Managers must make it clear to employees that it is their responsibility to influence management's perceptions of their work. If they make no effort to influence these perceptions and their supervisor has negative perceptions, the manager should never feel hesitant or uncomfortable telling them so.

If managers make on-the-spot corrections and hold counseling sessions when necessary to correct an employee's work, a negative review should never come as a surprise to the individual.

© 2009—Ed Rehkopf

Leadership on the Line
The Workbook

STAFF NOTES—

One of the most important things a supervisor can do to ensure meaningful employee development is to keep daily or weekly notes on the attitude, performance, and conduct of all employees under his supervision.

Staff Notes serve as a detailed and factual basis for informal discussions of an employee's performance and progress, for detailing specifics during performance reviews, and as backup and support for counseling and/or disciplinary actions.

All supervisors are encouraged to keep a small notebook for this purpose. The few minutes a day that it takes to record events, errors of omission and commission, attitude problems, superlative performance of duties, and conversations with or instructions to individual employees, will pay immense dividends in employees' development.

Such records allow a supervisor to identify and recognize outstanding employees, to discharge the problem employee without difficulty, and to develop each employee to his fullest potential through meaningful feedback.

© 2009—Ed Rehkopf

The Discussion

- Set the tone of the discussion during the meeting by restating the objectives and the role you and the employee will take in the discussion. Be informal, make the employee feel comfortable, and make sure you will not be interrupted.
- People want to know what the score is. Start by telling them the overall rating. Explain that the rating may change as the dialogue progresses. The rest of the review will focus on the elements that make up the rating. If they know the rating up front, they are more likely to participate and listen to what you have to say.
- During the discussion, be candid, sincere, and listen to the employee. Encourage a dialogue. The more an employee talks, the more he will remember and understand his part in the process.
- Be open to changing any of your criteria ratings if the employee provides convincing reasons why you should. Sometimes a supervisor's perceptions are based on faulty or partial information and a willingness to "be fair" may go a long way toward gaining the employee's trust, cooperation, and commitment.
- The performance review is a discussion about past performance. Its primary values are to recognize great performance and review opportunities for improvement. While this review is important and is the basis for an employee's overall score, the most productive review discussion should be focused on future performance and expectations. Typically a productive review discussion would focus more than half of the time on the future.
- Finalize the discussion by setting expectations and laying out specific goals to accomplish prior to the next review.

Documentation

- Fill out the performance review form thoroughly and accurately, reflecting the dialogue, your assessment of the employee's performance, and the agreed upon goals for improvement during the coming period.
- In a follow-up meeting, present him with the completed form, go over it with him, and ask him to sign the form.
- Give the employee a copy of the completed form and ensure the original goes in his personnel file.

While there may be areas of disagreement between you and the employee regarding his performance, it is ultimately your responsibility to rate him according to your standards and expectations, as well as your perceptions of how well he did. In other words, do not pull punches for the sake of agreement. If you do decide to give him the benefit of the doubt, make sure he understands that you are doing just that—but you still have reservations about his performance, and he will need to show improvement in the coming period

Applications

THE ANNUAL REVIEW—

Your supervisor calls you into his office, tells you to close the door and sit down at the chair in front of his desk. His demeanor is serious and you wonder what you've done wrong.

He then informs you it's time for your annual performance review. He hands you a completed form and tells you to read it. At the top a box labeled "Satisfactory" is checked. You scan down the page and see that he has scored you on 15 separate rating criteria.

This is the first you've heard about a review and no one has ever explained how your work is judged. Your head is swimming from trying to absorb so much information all at once. After scanning the sheet, you look up to see your supervisor's outstretched hand holding a pen.

"Any questions?" he asks. Somewhat bewildered, you shake your head no. "Good," he says, "just sign and date the form at the bottom." You comply and hand the form back to him. "That's all," he says rising from his chair. Dazed, you walk out of his office wondering what just happened.

© 2009—Ed Rehkopf

Exercise #6

While the narrative in the sidebar may be a worst case example, portions of this scenario are an all too familiar experience for many employees. Some of you may have even encountered a similar situation when your work was evaluated in your earliest work experiences. Take a few moments and think about the implications of such a review, how it made you feel, and its impact on your morale and motivation.

Why is it important to explain to an employee the criteria by which her work will be judged? And when should this be done?

_____
_____
_____
_____
_____
_____

When a supervisor hands you a completed evaluation form, what does this say to you and how does it make you feel?

_____
_____
_____
_____
_____
_____

As a conscientious employee, what are the most important things you want to know about the quality of your work? Why is it important for you to know these things?

_____
_____
_____
_____
_____
_____
_____

Leadership on the Line
The Workbook

"HIDDEN REASONS" YOUR EMPLOYEES LEAVE YOU—

Job not as expected. This is a prime reason for early departures.

Job doesn't fit talents and interests. Attributed to hasty hiring.

Little or no feedback/coaching. Give it honestly and often and you'll get job commitment, not just compliance.

No hope for career growth. The antidote: Provide talent self-management tools and training.

Feel devalued and unrecognized. Money issues appear here, but the category also includes even more employees who complained that no one ever said 'thanks' on the job or listened to what they had to say.

Feel overworked and stressed out. This comes from insufficient respect in the organization for the life/work balance of employees.

Lack of trust or confidence in leaders. Leaders have to understand that they're there to serve employees' needs, not the other way around. Develop leaders who care about and nurture their workers, and trust and confidence will develop as well."

Leigh Branham
Founder, Keeping the People, Inc., as reported by Business & Legal Reports

© 2009—Ed Rehkopf

Steps to Lower Employee Turnover

Study after study has demonstrated the high cost of employee turnover, particularly in the service industry where the work is so detail-intensive, requiring significant training to meet standards.

Recognizing that the desired outcome of every hiring decision is to find and bring aboard a qualified and enthusiastic person who will make a positive contribution to the success of the enterprise, it is essential that managers make every effort to lower employee turnover rates. Here are the requirements to help you do just that:

Interview Well. In addition to learning about the candidate's education, skills, and work experience, make sure you communicate to him the requirements of the position, including shifts, hours, and compensation, as well as your expectations and an honest assessment of the job, your company as a workplace, you as a boss, and the challenges you face in meeting customer expectations. The idea here is to ensure there will be no surprises for the employee once he starts working.

Hire Well. Use the techniques of Disciplined Hiring to screen applicants and check references. When possible, but consistently for all applicants, use personality assessments to ensure you put the right person in "the right seat on the bus."

Onboard Well. Use a variety of tools to both welcome and orient new hires to the workplace. An Employee Handbook, a Company Orientation, **and** a Departmental Orientation will provide and reinforce important information to the new hire. Managers must make sure both orientations are welcoming, consistent, and reinforcing, as well as making all necessary introductions to both supervisors and peers.

Train Well. Initial and ongoing training is essential. Most people want to do a good job and appreciate the efforts made to train them. Without adequate training and the necessary tools and resources to do their jobs well, new hires will quickly become cynical and alienated. This isn't good because their success guarantees your success.

Organize Well. No one wants to work in a chaotic environment. If your department or section is well-organized, if everyone knows where things are, if employees are well-trained in opening and closing procedures, if everyone knows their responsibilities and is held accountable, the workplace runs almost effortlessly. Don't run off good people by putting them through the hell of a disorganized operation.

Communicate Well. Daily interaction and direction ensures that everyone is informed, knows what is going on, and what they must do individually to accomplish the tasks at hand. It is also instrumental in building teamwork and a sense of shared mission and values. A Daily Huddle, or some other form of pre-shift meeting, is a necessary discipline to ensure ongoing, consistent communication.

Value Them. Remember the ultimate value of people in all you do. Value your employees and they will value you as a leader and their efforts at work.

The bottom line is that your leadership is the essential element in your success. If you have high levels of turnover, there is no one to blame but yourself.

Applications

Employee Empowerment

The aim of Service-Based Leadership is to empower employees at all levels to think and act in alignment with your company's values as they serve the needs of all constituencies—owners, customers, and other employees. Ultimately, employee empowerment is the end result of Service-Based Leadership.

Instead of the traditional view that employees are easily replaceable elements in an organization, people who must be trained to do narrow, well-defined tasks and who must be closely watched and supervised at all times, the concept of empowerment says that today's more educated and sometimes more sophisticated employees need and want to contribute more to their employer and workplace. Yet many businesses marginalize their employees by refusing to listen to them and by failing to let them contribute to the enterprise in any meaningful way.

Further, highly successful companies who engage their employees in developing work processes and continual process improvement have discovered that these empowered employees make indispensable partners in delivering service. Not only do they have a greater stake in the enterprise and are more fully committed to and responsible for their work, they actually equate their purpose and success with that of their company.

What is Employee Empowerment?

So what are empowered employees and how can they help your business meet its Mission and Vision? In the simplest terms **empowered employees are viewed as full-fledged partners** in your quest for high levels of quality and service. They are encouraged to think, act, and make decisions on their own based on guidelines defined by the company.

Leaders must understand that empowerment is not something bestowed on employees like some magical gift from management. The leaders' role is to establish both the environment and atmosphere where employees feel their empowerment and are emboldened to make decisions, knowing they have the support and backing of their leaders.

The major role that leaders make in empowering their employees is to create a culture where employees are valued and recognized as vital resources of the enterprise. They must also understand that to be successful with employee empowerment, **employees must fully sense the company's commitment to such empowerment**; simply saying that employees are empowered, does not make it so. Leaders at all levels must do more than talk the talk.

While employee empowerment may be seen as a desirable practice by management, it ultimately comes about **only with the recognition by employees that they are empowered**. This means that the focus of leaders must not be on what employees are doing to achieve empowerment, but on what they themselves are doing to promote and enable it.

EMPLOYEE EMPOWERMENT—

"Without empowerment, an organization will never be a service leader."

John Tschohl
Founder & President
Service Quality Institute

"A leader is great, not because he has power, but because of his or her ability to empower others."

John C. Maxwell
Developing the Leader Within You

© 2009—Ed Rehkopf

Leadership on the Line
The Workbook

The Distinction between Empowerment and Discretion

In discussing the need for written standards, policies, and procedures, we quoted Harvard Professor Theodore Levitt who said that "Discretion is the enemy of order, standardization, and quality." We have also talked about empowered employees being encouraged to think, act, and make decisions on their own based on guidance provided by the company. We offer the following to clarify what might seem a contradiction.

An important distinction to make for employees is that there is a hierarchy of rules to guide their empowered actions.

1. **Legal and liability issues** take precedence in that no employee may violate the law. This applies to many employment and labor laws such as Equal Employment Opportunity, the Fair Labor Standards Act, the Family Medical Leave Act, the Americans with Disabilities Act, the Occupational Safety and Health Act, and others.

2. For private clubs and some non-profit organizations there are the **policies based upon the by-laws and rules of the club or on tax laws**. Once again, no employee is authorized to modify or violate these rules which constitute the organizational or tax foundation of the enterprise.

3. Beyond these are the **organizational values** that define the company's culture of service and standards of behavior. These may not be altered at the employee's "discretion."

4. Next come the company's **operational policies** relating to its operating systems, such as human resources, accounting and financial management, and departmental operations.

5. Last are the **operational procedures** that describe how the routine things are done.

Since it's impossible to foresee every operational contingency, employees are authorized to alter procedures, even operational policies, when common sense and necessity dictate so long as their actions are in alignment with the law, club or non-profit rules, and the organization's values. When they do this, they should alert their leaders of their decisions and actions. It may well be that the employee's on-the-spot decision will point the way to improved performance. This is what makes employee empowerment so powerful. The people who do the work and interface directly with the customers are in a position to influence and improve the company's policies and procedures.

If leaders feel that an employee's action was inappropriate, this should be communicated in a supportive and non-critical way to the work team, as well as to the individual employee, so that all can learn from the experience.

EMPOWERMENT—

"Empowerment means feeling confident to act on your own authority. It means that your judgment is sufficiently respected by your leadership that they will support your decision. Should you make a mistake, that leadership will utilize it as an opportunity to teach a further point, not a chance to humiliate or berate you."

Patricia Aburdene and John Naisbitt
Megatrends for Women

"What is often called empowerment is really just taking off the chains and letting people loose. Credible leaders in this sense are liberators."

James M. Kouzes and Barry Z. Posner
Credibility

© 2009—Ed Rehkopf

Applications

NECESSITIES FOR EMPOWERMENT—

"First and foremost, strong leadership is an absolute necessity. Leaders must:

- *Embrace the principles of Service-Based Leadership.*
- *Be open with their employees.*
- *Be trusting and trusted.*
- *Be secure in themselves, their position, and their knowledge; not threatened by knowledgeable employees or those who show initiative.*
- *Be willing to share praise and shoulder blame.*
- *Be good communicators.*
- *Intrinsically understand and value the important role of line employees in the organization.*
- *Place a positive emphasis on problem discovery and solution.*
- *Allow their employees to demonstrate initiative and innovation, while giving them the 'freedom to fail' without repercussions."*

Ed Rehkopf
Making Employee Empowerment a Reality

© 2009—Ed Rehkopf

The Many Ways to "Kill" Empowerment

There are a number of ways to destroy employee empowerment, and none of them are caused by employees. If your employees do not feel empowered, look no further than your leadership and the way you interact with your people. In searching for reasons empowerment isn't working, focus on the following:

You haven't provided the "big picture" context of what your organization is trying to achieve. Your employees need to understand how their contribution furthers the basic aims of the organization. Defining and sharing your values and goals is a first step.

You've failed to give your employees the information and training they need to understand the context and scope of their empowerment. When you ask them to take on additional responsibilities as empowered employees, they need to understand why and what the benefits are for them as well as for you and the company. They will also need examples of what empowered behavior is. Lastly, they will need to know that they will not be blamed or punished for making mistakes.

You've given them guidelines, but then micromanage them. Maybe you've done a good job of defining limits, but then micromanage them. When you do this they will quickly understand that they are not "empowered" and that you will continue to make all the decisions, no matter how trivial.

You second guess their decisions. After giving your employees the guidelines to make empowered decisions, you criticize every decision they make. Put yourself in their shoes; how long would you put up with this before throwing in the towel on "employee empowerment"?

You have failed to give feedback on how your empowered employees are doing. Feedback, particularly early on, is critical so that employees understand by constant discussion and explanation what they are doing right and what can be improved on. Once they achieve a critical mass of understanding, they will feel more and more confident of their actions, will need less guidance, and will be looking for more and more ways to contribute.

You don't really understand what empowerment is. If you fail to realize that empowerment begins and ends with your leadership, if you think that empowerment is something your employees have to create, expecting your employees to act in empowered ways is a waste of time and energy.

You are only paying lip service to empowerment. Without your sincere commitment to your employees and their success, they will recognize your "empowerment" as a sham and will become more cynical and disaffected the more you try to encourage their "empowerment."

You have failed to value your employees. Without the most basic sense that they are valued and recognized as partners in your efforts to provide quality and service, they will recognize that your program of "empowerment" is just a way to manipulate them. People who think they are being manipulated are resentful and will be unresponsive to your continued exhortations to be "empowered."

CHARTING YOUR COURSE—

You may know where you want to go. But if you don't know where you are, you'll never get there from here.

Leadership on the Line
The Workbook

ASSESSMENTS—

In this section, you will be asked to do an assessment of the training you provide your employees.

You'll also be asked to think about all of the foregoing material in *The Workbook* and assess both former bosses and the way you interact with your employees. The purpose is to identify areas of your leadership and relationship skills that could be improved.

Lastly, you will be asked to develop a Leadership Plan to work on those areas you'd like to improve.

Training Assessment 84
Exercise #7 85
The Boss Assessment 86
The Personal Assessment 90
Your Leadership Assessment 91
Developing A Leadership Plan 93
Exercise #8 94

Leadership Assessments

Notes

Leadership on the Line
The Workbook — Assessments

Training Assessment

List the positions and approximate number of employees that you must train:

Positions	# of Employees
_____	_____
_____	_____
_____	_____
_____	_____

Do you have a training plan for your Dept / Section? ☐ Yes ☐ No

What are the primary means of training in your Dept / Section? (Check all that apply)

___ Written training manuals
___ Informal training by supervisor, i.e., OJT, demonstrations, etc.
___ Trailing more experienced employees
___ Training videos/DVDs
___ Role playing
___ Other: _____
___ Other: _____
___ Other: _____

What are the obstacles to training in your Dept /Section? (Check all that apply)

___ Low priority among many other competing requirements
___ Supervisors' other time commitments
___ Curriculum development
___ Lesson planning, preparation, and material
___ Training recordkeeping (administration)
___ Unbudgeted cost of employees' time for training
___ Other: _____
___ Other: _____
___ Other: _____

Do you have the necessary tools and equipment to train? (Check all that apply)

___ Adequate space—classroom, meeting room, or departmental area
___ AV equipment—projectors, computers
___ Desired or needed training videos/DVDs
___ Written training standards for each position
___ Other: _____
___ Other: _____
___ Other: _____

Rate your overall training effort (1 - 5, 1 being "poor," 5 being "outstanding") : _____

On the following page outline what steps you could take to improve training.

TRAINING—

Training is so important to the success of your operation that every leader must account for the quality of training he or she provides. This assessment is meant to provide an honest assessment of your efforts to train your employees. It will help you identify where your leadership and attention are needed.

© 2009—Ed Rehkopf

Leadership on the Line
The Workbook

Exercise #7

Outline what steps you would take within your department or section to improve the quality and consistency of the training you provide your employees.

THE HABIT OF EXCELLENCE—

"We are what we repeatedly do. Excellence, then, is not an act, but a habit."

Aristotle,
Greek Philosopher

© 2009—Ed Rehkopf

Assessments

THE BOSS ASSESSMENT—

We've all had many jobs in our lives. Some of us started by waiting tables or by working at a golf course. Many of us had hourly jobs in high school or as we worked our way through college. Think back to those earlier jobs and consider how you felt about them. Think about the hiring process—how you were treated and trained. What was your boss like? Did he make you feel welcomed? Did he motivate you to work hard? Were you treated as if you and your efforts mattered?

Now take the time to read each of the statements on the following pages as an employee contemplating your past bosses. Think about each statement in relation to your own work experiences. Rate how important each statement would be to you as an employee by placing an "x" on the line below the statement.

© 2009—Ed Rehkopf

The Boss Assessment

1. We are frequently recognized for our efforts.

2. I feel free to contribute my ideas and opinions, and they are valued.

3. The focus is always on problem solution, not placing blame.

4. My boss is smart and knows her business.

5. She treats all of us with respect.

6. He sets an example for all of us.

7. He tells us what he expects of us.

8. She cheerleads our efforts.

9. He motivates us to do our best.

10. She encourages us to think and gives us opportunities for personal growth.

11. We trust him to do what's right.

12. She treats us fairly and consistently; she doesn't play favorites.

Leadership on the Line
The Workbook

THE GLUE OF RELATIONSHIPS—

"The glue that holds all relationships together—including the relationship between the leader and the led—is trust, and trust is based upon integrity."

Brian Tracy
Motivational Author and Speaker

13. She acknowledges and gives us credit for our contributions.

Not important — Somewhat important — Very important

14. He takes the blame when something goes wrong.

Not important — Somewhat important — Very important

15. He makes things happen.

Not important — Somewhat important — Very important

16. She confronts inappropriate employee behavior.

Not important — Somewhat important — Very important

17. It's not all about him.

Not important — Somewhat important — Very important

18. He is focused on and committed to our company's success.

Not important — Somewhat important — Very important

19. He always has time for me and my co-workers.

Not important — Somewhat important — Very important

20. She listens to us and takes our ideas and concerns into account.

Not important — Somewhat important — Very important

21. He's always looking for a better way of doing things.

Not important — Somewhat important — Very important

22. She includes us in developing our department's plans.

Not important — Somewhat important — Very important

23. When he decides to do something, it gets done.

Not important — Somewhat important — Very important

24. He's a stand up guy. He always has our backs.

Not important — Somewhat important — Very important

25. He makes a point of talking to us every day.

Not important — Somewhat important — Very important

© 2009—Ed Rehkopf

Assessments

26. She keeps us informed about what's going on.
    Not important — Somewhat important — Very important

27. He keeps us informed of his whereabouts in case we need him.
    Not important — Somewhat important — Very important

28. He thanks us frequently for what we do.
    Not important — Somewhat important — Very important

29. She always makes a point of greeting us and introducing us to visitors.
    Not important — Somewhat important — Very important

30. We always feel appreciated.
    Not important — Somewhat important — Very important

31. Her door is always open to us.
    Not important — Somewhat important — Very important

32. He meets problems head on and finds a solution.
    Not important — Somewhat important — Very important

33. He's always enthusiastic and upbeat.
    Not important — Somewhat important — Very important

34. It's obvious that other managers look up to her and value her opinions.
    Not important — Somewhat important — Very important

35. He will not allow any team member to be belittled or marginalized.
    Not important — Somewhat important — Very important

36. She sets the bar high for all of us and we try to live up to her expectations.
    Not important — Somewhat important — Very important

37. His moral character is beyond reproach.
    Not important — Somewhat important — Very important

38. She makes us feel important, like we matter. We feel valued.
    Not important — Somewhat important — Very important

LEADERSHIP AND RELATIONSHIP—

"Because the personal relationship defines the existing quality of interpersonal interaction between the leader and would-be followers, followers will not join the leader without the requisite relationship. Leadership is the relationship."

Warren Blank
The 9 Natural Laws of Leadership

© 2009—Ed Rehkopf

Leadership on the Line
The Workbook

39. She explains the "big picture," connecting our daily tasks to the larger mission.

40. For once in my life I feel connected to a larger effort; it energizes me.

41. I actually look forward to coming to work.

42. She makes me want to do my best for her and the company.

43. He trains us well—I've never felt so confident or competent in my job.

44. I work in an well-organized operation; there's no chaos or confusion.

45. I was impressed by my treatment during hiring. I couldn't wait to start.

46. I have complete confidence in her.

47. She has well-defined standards of service and behavior for us.

48. He is strict, but fair in enforcing his standards.

49. She gives us all the tools, training, resources, and support to do our jobs.

50. I really love my job.

COMMON DECENCIES—

"Little kindnesses and courtesies are important. In relationships, the little things are the big things."

Stephen R. Covey
Bestselling Author

© 2009—Ed Rehkopf

Assessments

The Personal Assessment

Unfortunately there is no "ideal" leader. We each have our strengths and weaknesses in how we relate to others, but by becoming aware of those areas needing improvement, we can focus on the attitudes, skills, and techniques we need to better serve our employees.

Having completed the "Boss Assessment" exercise, give some thought to how your employees might rate you in relation to those same statements. Go back through the previous exercise and rate each statement as if you were your own employee and were considering how the statements applied to you as a leader. Place an "o" on the line under each statement indicating how you think your employees might rate you.

Recognizing how important some statements were to you as an employee, see if the way you interact with your employees meets your own sense of what is important. The key here is to give an honest assessment about how you relate to your employees. You may do very well on some and poorly on others.

After you've finished, go back and look for those statements where there is a wide gap between what's important to you as an employee (marked with an "x") and how your employees would rate you (marked with an "o"). The statements with the largest discrepancies are the areas you need to focus on in developing your leadership and relationship skills.

If you really want to know how you are viewed by your employees, make copies of the Boss Assessment and ask them to fill it out anonymously and return it to you. For them to be completely frank with you, though, they must trust you implicitly. Even then, some may be uncomfortable rating their boss' leadership skills. In this case, you must devise a way to ensure their anonymity. A good approach might be to have the Human Resources Manager or some other trusted individual distribute the assessment and receive them when completed. This individual would then pass them on to you without revealing who completed and turned them in.

Keep in mind that your purpose here is to strengthen your leadership skills and abilities. Your employees, by being honest with you about their feelings, are doing you an immense favor. Should some or all rate you poorly, don't be tempted to "kill the messenger." Use their feedback to do some soul-searching and commit yourself to changing what you can—your approach to leadership and how you relate to your followers.

THE BOSS vs. THE LEADER

"The boss drives his workers; the leader coaches them.

The boss depends on authority; the leader on goodwill.

The boss inspires fear; the leader inspires enthusiasm.

The boss says 'I'; the leader, 'we.'

The boss fixes the blame for the breakdown; the leader fixes the breakdown.

The boss knows how it is done; the leader shows how.

The boss says, 'Go'; the leader says, 'Let's go!'"

Robert C. Maxwell
Developing the Leader Within You

© 2009—Ed Rehkopf

Leadership on the Line
The Workbook

Your Leadership Assessment

YOUR LEADERSHIP ASSESSMENT—

The chart at right and on the following page indicates for each assessment statement where you have a discrepancy and those areas of your leadership and relationship skills that need work.

You can then use this recognition of where work is needed in developing your Leadership Plan.

#	Statement	Items to Review and Focus On		
1	We are frequently recognized for our efforts.	Leadership Values	Principles of Empl Relations	Value Your People
2	I feel free to contribute my ideas and opinions, and they are valued.	Employee Empowerment	Value Your People	Service-Based Leadership
3	The focus is always on problem solution, not placing blame.	Leadership Values	Principles of Empl Relations	Empowerment
4	My boss is smart and knows her business.	Trust	Competency	Leadership Applications
5	She treats us all with respect.	Leadership Values	Principles of Empl Relations	Value Your People
6	He sets an example for all of us.	Leadership Values	Managers' Code of Ethics	Leadership Principles
7	He tells us what he expects of us.	Leadership Values	Principles or Empl Relations	Communication
8	She cheerleads our efforts.	Motivation	Morale	Communication
9	He motivates us to do our best.	Motivation	Morale	Communication
10	She encourages us to think and gives us opportunities for personal growth.	Employee Empowerment	Value Your People	Leadership Principles
11	We trust him to do what's right.	Do the Right Thing	Trust	Relationships
12	She treats us fairly and consistently; she doesn't play favorites.	Leadership Values	Mgmt Professionalism	
13	She acknowledges and gives us credit for our contributions.	Leadership Values	Principles of Empl Relations	Communication
14	He takes the blame when something goes wrong.	Personal Responsibility	Do the Right Thing	Trust
15	He makes things happen.	Will to Make Things Happen	Personal Responsibility	Do the Right Thing
16	She confronts inappropriate employee behavior	Standards	Accountability	Do the Right Thing
17	It's not all about him.	Ego	Leadership Basics	
18	He is focused on and committed to our company's success.	Level 5 Leadership	Leadership Basics	Managers' Code of Ethics
19	He always has time for me and my co-workers.	Communication	Employee Engagement	
20	She listens to us and takes our ideas and concerns into account.	Communication	Employee Engagement	Value Your People
21	He's always looking for a better way of doing things.	Continual Improvement	Leadership Applications	Service-Based Leadership
22	She includes us in developing our department's plans.	Planning	Employee Engagement	Value Your People
23	When he decides to do something, it gets done.	Will to Make Things Happen	Leadership Basics	
24	He's a stand up guy. He always has our backs.	Do the Right Thing	Personal Responsibility	Leadership Basics
25	He makes a point of talking to us every day.	Engagement	Communication	

© 2009—Ed Rehkopf

Assessments

Your Leadership Assessment, Continued

	Statement	Items to Review and Focus On	
26	She keeps us informed about what's going on.		
	Communication	Leadership Basics	
27	He keeps us informed of his whereabouts in case we need him.		
	Communication	Principles of Empl Relations	Value Your People
28	He thanks us frequently for what we do.		
	Feedback	Principles of Empl Relations	Value Your People
29	She always makes a point of greeting us and introducing us to visitors.		
	Value Your People		
30	We always feel appreciated.		
	Value Your People	Principles of Empl Relations	
31	Her door is always open to us.		
	Communication	Engagement	Value Your People
32	He meets problems head on and finds a solution.		
	Will to Make Things Happen	Leadership Basics	
33	He's always enthusiastic and upbeat.		
	Sets Example	Leadership Basics	Principles of Empl Relations
34	It's obvious that other managers look up to her and value her opinions.		
	Competency	Leadership Applications	
35	He will not allow any team member to be belittled or marginalized.		
	Engagement	Value Your People	
36	She sets the bar high for all of us and we try to live up to her expectations.		
	Standards	Accountability	
37	His moral character is beyond reproach.		
	Sets Example	Managers' Code of Ethics	Mgmt Professionalism
38	She makes us feel important, like we matter. We feel valued.		
	Value Your People		
39	She explains the "big picture," connecting our daily tasks to the larger mission.		
	Communication	Morale	Motivation
40	For once in my life I feel connected to a larger effort; it energizes me.		
	Employee Empowerment	Need to Serve	Motivation
41	I actually look forward to coming to work.		
	Morale	Motivation	
42	She makes me want to do my best for her and the company.		
	Motivation		
43	He train us well - I've never felt so confident or competent in my job.		
	Training	Leadership Applications	Leadership Basics
44	I work in a well-organized operation; there's no chaos or confusion.		
	Competency	Planning	
45	I was impressed by my treatment during hiring. I couldn't wait to start.		
	Hiring	Value Your People	Motivation
46	I have complete confidence in her.		
	Trust	Relationship	Leadership Basics
47	He makes me understand how my efforts count.		
	Motivation	Employee Empowerment	
48	She has well-defined standards of service and behavior for us.		
	Culture	Standards	Accountability
49	She gives us all the tools, training, resources, and support to do our jobs.		
	Leadership Basics	Training	Employee Empowerment
50	I really love my job.		
	Morale	Motivation	

THE TOP 10 LEADERSHIP QUALITIES—

1. *Vision*
2. *Integrity*
3. *Dedication*
4. *Magnanimity*
5. *Humility*
6. *Openness*
7. *Creativity*
8. *Fairness*
9. *Assertiveness*
10. *Sense of Humor*

David Hakala

© 2009—Ed Rehkopf

Leadership on the Line
The Workbook

THE GOLDEN RULE—

The golden rule is usually associated with Christianity. But other religions have versions of it also. Then there are individuals who live by it, regardless of faith.

Whether or not people live by their moral codes, religious or not, is another issue. But here are some quotes that show at least the concept is there:

Commonsensism: *A version of the golden rule put into modern, non-religious terms that some people live by is, 'Treat people the way you'd like to be treated.'*

Buddhism: *560 BC - 'Hurt not others with that which pains yourself.'*

Judaism: *1300 BC - 'Thou shalt Love thy neighbor as thyself.'*

Hinduism: *3200 BC - 'One should always treat others as they themselves wish to be treated.'*

Zoroastrianism: *600 BC - 'Whatever is disagreeable to yourself, do not do unto others.'*

Confucianism: *557 BC - 'What you do not want done to yourself, do not do to others.'*

Christianity: *30 AD— 'Whatsoever ye would that others should do to you, do ye even so to them.'"*

Golden Rule Organization

© 2009—Ed Rehkopf

Developing A Leadership Plan

Having identified those areas of your leadership and relationship skills that need work, develop a specific plan to strengthen weak areas.

Example: If the assessment indicates you need to focus on Leadership Basics, draw up a list of things you can do to improve.

1. Ask a respected leader to mentor you, specifically in those areas you've found you need work.
2. Re-read *Leadership on the Line* making note of specific things you can do to improve your relationship and communication skills or improve the trust between you and your constituencies, particularly your employees.
3. Read other books in the Bibliography to reinforce and expand on those ideas in *Leadership on the Line*.
4. Prepare flash cards with quotes or lists from these books to keep prominently on your desk as a reminder of things you need to focus on.
5. Establish a schedule of meetings with your staff to identify problems, brainstorm solutions, and plan for implementation.
6. Make a greater effort to keep your employees informed and continually ask them to do the same regarding problems they encounter in their jobs.
7. Meet privately with each of your team members to discuss what they like and dislike about their jobs and what obstacles they face.
8. Act decisively to remove those obstacles.
9. Engage with your staff daily.
10. Make efforts to be more sensitive to the needs, challenges, and feelings of others.
11. Monitor the manner in which you interact with your staff and keep a notebook of your feelings about and reactions to events, issues, and incidents in your section. Often writing these down will help you pinpoint areas of conflict, communication issues, and problems of motivation and morale. As a leader, it's up to you to fix these challenges, but you need to consider deeply the causes of the problems as they may point back to the quality of your leadership.
12. Give your employees regular feedback and thank them often.
13. Recognize the importance of your employees to the success of the company and to you as their leader. Ensure you sincerely value them as individuals and let them know it by your words and actions.
14. Brainstorm with other respected leaders who are familiar with your leadership style and operation. Their outside view may be clearer than yours from the inside.

Leadership development is a lifelong pursuit. You cannot change yourself overnight. But the more you work at learning and demonstrating Service-Based Leadership skills, the more your constituencies will respond favorably to your leadership and the more success you will achieve.

Assessments

Exercise #8

Make a priority list of those areas where you need to work on your leadership skills and abilities.

_____

DEVELOPING YOUR PLAN—

You have come a long way with this course. Now is the time to put what you've learned into action. Draw up a plan to develop or enhance your leadership skills. Then be persistent in following your plan. It is only through the application of your "will to make it happen" that your success will be won.

Now draw up a list of specific things you will do to develop those skills and abilities.

_____

FOLLOWING YOUR PLAN—

"Setting a goal is not the main thing. It is deciding how you will go about achieving it and staying with that plan."

Tom Landry
Legendary Dallas Cowboy Coach

© 2009—Ed Rehkopf

Leadership on the Line
The Workbook — Conclusion

GETTING TO WORK

Having read *Leadership on the Line* and worked through this *Workbook*, you should have an excellent understanding of the basics of leadership. The task now is to use what you've learned to build strong and abiding relationships with your various constituencies.

If you have a lot to work on, don't think you need to improve everything at once. Take your time and focus on a limited number of key leadership initiatives. When you've made progress on these, set your sights on your next priorities. The key is to make continual improvements. The more progress you make in developing your skills as a Service-Based Leader, the more your followers will respond and the more success you'll achieve.

LAST THOUGHTS

While we have covered a lot of ground and discussed a lot of leadership principles, attributes, and disciplines, keep the following foremost in mind:

1. The quality of your leadership is determined by the **influence** you have with your followers, which, in turn, is established by the quality of your **relationships** with them—and your relationships are built on a foundation of **trust**, of which **integrity**, **competency**, **consistency**, and **common decency** are primary ingredients.

2. As you progress through your career and assume greater authority and responsibilities, you will find it helpful to periodically remind yourself of leadership basics by reviewing *Leadership on the Line* and *The Workbook*. Even after a forty year career, I still find it helpful to return to this foundation.

3. All of Jim Collins' *Good to Great* leaders possessed the qualities of Level 5 Leadership, a paradoxical blend of personal humility and a fanatical zeal for the success of their enterprise. I believe that Service-Based Leadership is the first step toward achieving those qualities.

4. Never stop learning and always be open to the never-ending lessons around you. Even bad examples and failure can be powerful instructors.

5. Care for and sincerely value people. While there are many avenues to success in life, every one, except that of a successful hermit, requires that you recognize the ultimate value of people in all you do.

6. You owe it to those who come after you to pass on your life lessons and hard won wisdom. The world will always need Service-Based Leaders and, unfortunately, they are in short supply. While your example will be the best teacher, a formal structure of leadership basics is a critical starting point.

Thank you for your interest and effort in making this journey. I trust that it will lead to success in your career, as well as in life. Best wishes and good luck in all your endeavors!

Ed Rehkopf

LET SERVICE BEGIN WITH YOU—

"In attempting to affect positive change in your company, do not wait for others to do their part. Whether your boss or your peers believe in or apply the principles of Service-Based Leadership, make your contribution by taking the initiative. In time, your example will have an unmistakable impact on all around you."

Leadership on the Line

© 2009—Ed Rehkopf

Notes

Leadership on the Line
The Workbook

Bibliography

I recommend the following books as ones that helped me as I learned to develop my leadership skills and abilities. This is by no means an exhaustive list and there are many other fine books available to help you improve as a manager and leader; and new ones are being published every year.

Made to Stick
Chip Heath and Dan Heath, Random House, New York, 2007

Leadership on the Line: A Guide for Front Line Supervisors, Business Owners, and Emerging Leaders, 2d Edition
Ed Rehkopf, Clarity Publications, Mooresville, NC, 2006

Purple Cow: Transform your Business by Being Remarkable
Seth Godin, Penguin Books, NY, 2003

What Winners Do To Win!
Nicki Joy, John Wiley & Sons, Hoboken, NJ, 2003

Good to Great, Why Some Companies Make the Leap . . . and Others Don't
Jim Collins, HarperCollins, New York, 2001

Fish! A Remarkable Way to Boost Morale and Improve Results
Stephen K. Lundin, Harry Paul, John Christensen, Hyperion, NY, 2000

Topgrading, How Leading Companies Win by Hiring, Coaching, and Keeping the Best People
Bradford D. Smart, Ph.D., Prentice Hall Press, New York, 1999

The E-Myth Revisited, Why Most Small Businesses Don't Work and What to Do About It
Michael E. Gerber, HarperCollins, New York, 1995

Developing the Leader Within You
John C. Maxwell, Nelson Business, New York, 1993

The 7 Habits of Highly Effective People
Stephen R. Covey, Simon and Schuster, New York, 1989

At America's Service, How Corporations Can Revolutionize the Way They Treat Their Customers
Karl Albrecht, Dow Jones-Irwin, Homewood IL, 1988

The Game of Work, How to Enjoy Work as Much as Play
Charles A. Coonradt with Lee Nelson, Liberty Press, Orem UT, 1984

In Search of Excellence
Thomas J. Peters and Robert H. Waterman, Jr., Warner Books, New York, 1982

A Message to Garcia
Elbert Hubbard, Peter Pauper Press, Inc., White Plains, NY. 1977

Try Giving Yourself Away
David Dunn, The Updegraff Press, Ltd., Scarsdale, NY, 1947

PROFESSIONAL READING—

*"The more that you read,
The more things you will know.
The more that you learn,
The more places you'll go."*

Dr. Seuss
(Theodor Geisel)
American Author and Cartoonist

THE LEADER IS BEST—

"The Leader is best,

When people are hardly aware of his existence,

Not so good when people praise his government,

Less good when people stand in fear,

Worst, when people are contemptuous.

Fail to honor people, and they will fail to honor you.

But of a good leader, who speaks little

When his work is done, his aim fulfilled,

The people say, 'We did it ourselves.'"

Lao Tzu
Chinese philosopher

About the Author

Ed Rehkopf is a graduate of the U.S. Military Academy and received a Masters of Professional Studies degree in Hospitality Management from Cornell's School of Hotel Administration. During his long and varied career, he has managed two historic, university-owned hotels, managed at a four-star desert resort, directed operations for a regional hotel chain, opened two golf and country clubs, worked in golf course development, and launched a portal web site for the club industry.